Developmental
MANAGEMENT

FOUNDATIONS OF BUSINESS

Developmental Management

General Editor: Ronnie Lessem

Charting the Corporate Mind*
Charles Hampden-Turner

Managing in the Information Society
Yoneji Masuda

Developmental Management
Ronnie Lessem

Foundations of Business
Ivan Alexander

* This edition not available in the USA.

Developmental
MANAGEMENT

Foundations of Business

ENTERPRISE, TECHNOLOGY, SOCIETY

IVAN ALEXANDER

WITH A FOREWORD BY
RONNIE LESSEM

Basil Blackwell

Copyright © Ivan Alexander 1990;
Foreword © Ronnie Lessem 1990

First published 1990

Basil Blackwell Ltd
108 Cowley Road, Oxford, OX4 1JF, UK

Basil Blackwell, Inc.
3 Cambridge Center
Cambridge, Massachusetts 02142, USA

All rights reserved. Except for the quotation of short passages for the purposes of criticism and review, no part of this publication may be reproduced, stored in a retrieval system, or transmitted, in any form or by any means, electronic, mechanical, photocopying, recording or otherwise, without the prior permission of the publisher.

Except in the United States of America, this book is sold subject to the condition that it shall not, by way of trade or otherwise, be lent, re-sold, hired out, or otherwise circulated without the publisher's prior consent in any form of binding or cover other than that in which it is published and without a similar condition including this condition being imposed on the subsequent purchaser.

British Library Cataloguing in Publication Data

A CIP catalogue record for this book is available from the British Library.

Library of Congress Cataloging in Publication Data

Alexander, Ivan.
Foundations of business:
enterprise, technology, society / Ivan Alexander.
p. cm.
Includes bibliographical references.
ISBN 0-631-17718-3
1. Industry–Social aspects. 2. Business ethics.
3. Business–History. I. Title.
HD60.A39 1990
658.4'08–dc20   89-17680 CIP

Typeset in 11 on 13 pt Ehrhardt
by Hope Services (Abingdon) Ltd.
Printed in Great Britain by
William Clowes, Beccles, Suffolk

Contents

Foreword by Ronnie Lessem — ix
Preface — xvii
Introduction — 1

PART I   PRESENT

Section 1   Attributes of Business — 5

Preamble — 5

1 Personal Attributes in Business — 9
Entrepreneurship and Autonomy — 9
Leadership and Management — 13
Enterprise and Wisdom — 15
Judgement and the Making of Decisions — 16

2 Value Attributes in Enterprise — 19
Price and Value — 19
The Architecture of Price — 21

3 Attributes of Marketing — 23
Legends of Salesmanship — 23
Salesmen – Born or Made — 26
The Art of Negotiation — 28

4 Business and the Attributes of Taxation — 33
The Ways of Taxation — 33
Tax and Motives — 35

Section 2 Politics and Business 41
Preamble 41

5 Politics around Business 45
Politics and Business 45
The Democracy of Money 47
Politics and Capitalism 48
Politics and Communism 49
The Soviet Union and the Future of Business 51

6 Politics in Business 55
Politics and Generosity 55
Politics and Conservation 56
Politics and Reform 57
Liberty, Privacy and Property 58

PART II PAST

Section 3 Movements that Shaped Business 63
Preamble 63

7 Freedom and Accountability 69
Freedom as Trust 69
Honour above Honesty 71

8 Mercantilists and Adventurers 75
The Rise of Mercantilism 75
Merchant-Adventurers: the Dutch 77

9 Industry and Society 81
Gold and the Privilege of Kings 81
The Age of Steam 83
Man and Machine 85

Section 4 Ideas that Shaped Business 89
Preamble 89

10 Christianity and Enterprise 91
The Idea of Work 91
The Idea of Rational Speculation 94
The Idea of Usury 95

Missing Links of Rationality	97
'The Acres Melting'	104
11 Capitalism and Enterprise	107
The Transnationalism of Money	107
Capitalism, the Reformation and the Protestant Ethic	109
The Coming of Free Enterprise	112

Section 5   Cultures that Shaped Business   119

Preamble	119
12 The Jews: A Dispersed Culture	121
The Business Outsiders	121
Usury, Persecution and Competition	123
13 The Japanese: A Clustered Culture	127
A Sun Lately Risen	127
The Industrial Revolution in Japan	129
The Mind of Japan	131
Status and the Japanese	134
14 Civility in Business Enterprise	137
Manners Maketh Man	137
Civility in Business Enterprise	139
The Westering of Japan	142

PART III   FUTURE

Section 6   Business in the Age of Information   149

Preamble	149
15 People, Computers and Business	153
Computers and Business	153
Meeting a Computer	154
Computers and Eternity	155
Computers and Information	157
Computers and Knowledge	159
Computers and Being	162
16 Business, Computers and Society	167
A Symbol of the Age of Information	167

An Extension of Man	169
Production and Service	170

Section 7 Business in Society — 175
Preamble — 175

17 Business and Civilization — 183
Culture and Government — 183
Exchange and Natural Instinct — 186

Epilogue — 191

Index — 193

Foreword

It is not often that we stop to reflect on the 'Foundations of Business'. Yet where would a house be without its foundations? A house or business without foundations lacks stability, continuity and identity. Yet how many business and management courses are run without ever questioning or even considering the foundations of business?

Interestingly enough it is usually only the mature person who returns to his or her roots, and hence it is the mature manager who returns to the foundations of business. We need experience and the perspective of space and time before we are able to observe living things from sufficient distance to describe their inner workings. Henry James, perhaps the greatest American psychologist of all time, observed at the turn of the century how great an undertaking business is at its best. However, he lamented, the great novelists chose not to write about business and the great businessmen were not writers.

Times, in that respect, have not changed. The great contemporary novelists have not focused their attentions on the unfolding drama of business. Meanwhile the business media continually concentrate on some actual or would-be takeover, in which protagonist and antagonist inveigh against one another.

The result is that the whole business story is never told. On the one hand academics have monopolized the analytically based functions of business. On the other hand, at least in more recent years, successful businessmen like Lee Iacocca in the US, Roland Petit in France, and John Harvey Jones in Britain have written prodigiously about the fruits of their endeavours. However, the roots and core of business have seldom been revealed. Henry Ford in the US has been the isolated exception, and now Ivan Alexander follows in his footsteps.

What are the foundations, then, with which business people like Henry Ford and Ivan Alexander are concerned? To some extent they are personal, rooted within the psyche of the individual. To some extent they are historical, rooted in the economic, political, cultural and religious development of whole societies. Finally, they are also technological, rooted within the advance of business from a material base to an information base.

We now turn to Ivan Alexander, one of those rare businessmen who is also a gifted writer.

Ivan Alexander was born in East Prussia, in 1923, into Europe's troubled times. After a standard British schooling, he pursued a varied further education. It included a spell of science at Edinburgh University and a few months of Russian studies at Manchester. He then served in the infantry, first as a corporal in a Scottish Lowland regiment, then as an officer in a Highland one, until the end of the war, when he was attached to a political division of the Allied Control Commission in Germany. There he not only saw the revival of German democracy, but also met and befriended such statesmen as Konrad Adenauer and Kurt Schumacher.

In 1949, having read Politics, Philosophy and Economics at Oxford, he hoped to become a journalist but failed to find an opening. He went into business instead, as a trader, buying steel for India from Europe. He visited, in fact, nearly every steel mill, both large and small, in Eastern and Western Europe. As a result, and in close succession, Ivan Alexander was exposed to the foundations of business from the academic heights of Oxford and from the commercial depths of London's City. Business, for him, was eminently personal, eminently social and eminently political.

India ran out of foreign exchange in the 1950s, and the trading company for which Alexander worked was dissolved. By then he had learnt two lessons: that a bazaar mentality is unsuitable for continuing business, and that one must get to know suppliers personally, because selling decisions are as much a product of sellers' outlook as they are a product of their factories. Hence Alexander uncovered the personal foundations of business. Moreover, when India ran out of money, and his company was dissolved, he realized that a corporation's security lies precariously balanced in the scales of international affairs. Hence he uncovered the economic and political foundations of business.

As a seasoned businessman, Alexander's initial approach to the foundations of business is not economic or administrative but personal. Even big businesses, for him, are constellations of discernible individual identities. What makes the difference between one business and another is the quality of the people in each identifiable cluster and the affinity they have with those in other clusters. The enduring passion of businessmen is not, as many outsiders believe, profit, but achievement. Businessmen mind their money, of course, and value it for what it brings, but they also value it as a measuring rod of achievement. Moreover, because businessmen have a vision, they have to take risks – political, social and psychological, as well as economic risks. For Alexander, such a vision is sometimes taken to the point of perfection, rather than good sense and good profits.

Business, at root, is always a blend of fact and value. Price, for a practising business philosopher like Alexander, is not the point at which supply profitably meets demand, but an attempt to join fact with value. Price is a scale for the value of things for which there is no other measure. It is to an economy what justice is to the law. Behind price, the basic brick, is an architecture of value. It is the architecture, Alexander says, of that gigantic sorting mechanism which is capitalism. It does not allocate compassion, justice or brotherly love, but it allocates resources extremely well.

Capitalists, operating in the marketplace, like to be thought of as doers. Most of the time they are talkers. Some of the time they are thinkers. A few of them, according to Alexander, are listeners. At negotiations, so much part of the market scene, they must also be actors, because even sober negotiation is at heart a drama. Subsequent to the drama of negotiation – that personal ingredient amidst the impersonal marketplace – as after a good meal, it is best to leave replete, but not sated. The architecture of value, then, is a blend of personal expression and impersonal machination.

In fact individualism, Keynes tells us, if it can be purged of its defects and abuses, is the best safeguard of personal liberty in the sense that, compared with any other system, it greatly widens the field for the exercise of personal choice. It is also the best safeguard for the variety of life.

This variety, according to Keynes, preserves the traditions which embody the most secure and successful choices of former generations, and, being the handmaid of experiment, is the most powerful instrument to improve the future. In the final analysis it is better to let a hundred flowers bloom than to grow one that is perfect. If there is only one flower, in fact, you cannot tell that it is perfect.

Businessmen, according to Alexander, cannot help becoming

worldly philosophers. They are world-immersed. They sense the moods of time and commerce. A point of view develops. What other occupations, he asks, are better suited to reflection? Not that of theologians, for their reference is to quite another world. Not that of philosophers who rearrange the meaning of truth from time to time to give eternity a dusting. Not that of politicians who have to choose between the things they would themselves elect, and the public that elects them. Not that of gossip columnists and social diarists; they concern themselves with a floating world.

The market does not wish to be judged; it wishes to be used. That may not be justice. It just is. Therefore capitalism, for Alexander, is not a system but a critical procedure. It is a testing ground for what can, and what cannot be done with money, knowledge and imagination. It is a continuous critique which has success as its judge and society as its jury. Business life asks, every day, for self-discovery and self-examination. In it there is a continuous evolution of beliefs, ideas, tastes, arts and inventions. Businessmen must be a yeast and a leaven, and provide enough of it to make the national loaf a bread and not a pancake.

Alexander maintains that Gorbachev's mind, more than that of any Western statesman, is a business mind. It seeks sober results bereft of delusion. It is determined to make the future profitable. It is prepared to write off losses. Gorbachev's new vision has the goodwill of all Western nations.

On balance Western-style democracy, using the business system to unfold the productive talents of people, has proved – in Alexander's opinion and perhaps in Gorbachev's – the most agreeable society to live and work in. Energy and talent, and the right to their display, are worthy assets of mankind. They are also worthy assets of Ivan Alexander.

Alexander's life and management style, at least until his late forties, mirrored that of the transnational manager of today. In 1967 Alexander moved to Los Angeles and, slowly, learnt the meaning of work. He was asked to set up and be President (as well as office boy) of the first oil pipe distributing company in Southeast Asia. The company had a former Governor of California as its Chairman.

Living in Singapore and Jakarta in 1973 and at the age of nearly 50, with a wife, three children and $16,000, Alexander started his own business in Indonesia, supplying international oil companies with pipe. Within a year he had moved to New Jersey, USA, to continue his business. Over the course of eight years the company captured 5.8 per cent of the global drill pipe market outside the USA. At the age of 61, Alexander, now resident in Switzerland, sold his business to a Swiss company, with whom he has since remained on friendly terms, and returned to the writing career of which he had dreamed some thirty-five years earlier.

The conduct of business, on a global scale, has gradually evolved from mercantilism to modern transnationalism. In the process the conduct of business has become, in a discernible sense, more human. For example, compare large-scale business today with that in Christopher Columbus's day. 'One who has gold,' observed Columbus, 'does as he wills in the world, and it even sends souls to Paradise.' In a little more than a century the Indian population of Mexico was reduced by 90 per cent, in the name of both commercial gain and religious righteousness.

Early capitalism, in fact, was an age of strict reason, but little reasonableness. Whereas the medieval world had explained the existence of beggars by the working of God's mysterious will, the nineteenth century explained that beggars existed by the working of economic laws. To the Middle Ages, and the age of mercantilism, property had been tangible things, things that do not beget other things: land, gold, treasure, saintly relics. In the eighteenth century, however, money and property came to be seen as fertile, as begetting seed. Money could make money could make money.

In fact our present age, Alexander maintains, is the only one we have ever known in which unlimited growth has been a realistic vision. So the world has found its economic mission. Ideologies have grown which take boundlessness for granted: the inevitability of progress, the perfectibility of man, popular democracy, the pursuit of happiness, Marxism and Socialism, free enterprise and free trade.

Alexander focuses on two particular cultures that have shaped free enterprise, in highly contrasting terms in recent times – the Jews and the Japanese. The Jews he cites as 'a dispersed culture'. Whereas the capitalism of Catholic bankers and Nonconformist Protestants was a capitalism of the structure, their capitalism was one of the gaps. For the Jews, through the centuries, have been dispersed amongst nations, across all four quarters of the globe, and have operated on the margins of society by both necessity and choice. The Jews, from antiquity to modern times, breathed the spirit of their holy Book as much as they breathed the air of their country of sojourn. In exile, they were a people governed by a sacred code and by sacred hopes. The land of their Messiah and the landscape of Zion was a vision, against which any real landscape – Alexander tells us – paled into mere territoriality. Such an inward arrangement of reality encouraged the mind to combine and recombine, an ability which is the mark of the entrepreneur.

While the Jews are a dispersed, entrepreneurial people the Japanese are a managerial, clustered one. The essence of Japan's commercial philosophy, Alexander maintains, is to keep the country going, to keep people employed, and to allow investment and modernization to continue. By this means Japan has turned Marx's critique of capitalism against Marx himself. Marx contended that the capitalist skims the surplus value – the difference between the worker's wage and the value the worker produces – for the capitalist's own profit. So, on the face of it, does the Japanese capitalist, but with a twist that Marx did not foresee: that the Japanese corporation would immediately turn the money back into investments for the further benefit of managers and employees.

So Marx's understanding of the relationship between the technological, economic and civil foundations of business was flawed. By the time Alexander had reached his age of wisdom he was able to see this clearly.

While Alexander co-authored a book on a branch of business, *Selling Industrial Products*, in the sixties, and lectured to the American Management Association in the seventies, it is now, in his third age, that he has acquired the insight and the wisdom to reflect upon business's very foundations. Such foundations, for Alexander, are not only personal and political, from a present perspective, but also economic, social and religious, from a historical perspective, and technological and civil, from a futurist perspective. The present half-century, according to Alexander, has seen changes in business and the world economy which will carry us into the next century. The greatest of these changes has been the new meanings given to the classic, late eighteenth-century economic theory of the international division of labour. This theory advocated the global benefits of letting each country supply to others that which it could produce most cheaply.

The theory now redefines itself in several ways. Beside the 'cheapest' division, that is the international division of labour, we have an international division of management effectiveness, an international division of fashion preferences, an international division of quality preferences, and an international division of currency and interest rate preferences. Japan's success, for example, has been primarily due to managerial effectiveness.

Such effectiveness has been particularly evident in the high technology sector, where human assets are at a premium, and where an information-centred and future-oriented society, like the Japanese one, has a cultural advantage. Computer programs, for example, are eternal. This seems to distinguish computer software from other inventions of man. Like civilization itself, there is no limit to what can be added to it. Write a word processing program, for example, as a core. Add to it a dictionary to check the spelling of words. Then add to it voice recognition. It is the first product humanity has devised which has some measure of eternity; it cannot be consumed by use.

Like computer hardware and software, production and services are a continuum. It is one of the delusions of our day, Alexander maintains, that manufacturing is in retreat. We have not become a post-industrial society; we have not even begun to be one in any real sense. We live, instead, in an age in which almost every activity, from making maps to playing games, is a prospect for industrialization. Business and life are ever more strongly interconnected.

In conclusion Alexander argues that business is a friend of civilization, just so long as it does not seek to create its own. The continued expansion of business is no danger to the world, if it is part of the expansion of the valuable world. Its financial power is not likely to overwhelm hopes of a lively and gentle life, if it is itself hopeful of such a life. Its values are not divorced from, or in opposition to, other, non-commercial values of mankind, if it forswears an arrogance of power.

In that concluding argument Alexander endorses the underlying and fundamentally human purpose of developmental management. Business, in effect, is not a means to its own end, but to a personal, economic and civil one. Whereas at the early stages of the development of a business, both historically and commercially, this may not be apparent, it becomes steadily more evident as the enterprise, and the social and economic environment around it, mature.

Ronnie Lessem
London, 1990

Preface

Business is a profession without a strong sense of profession. It has little historical awareness of its becoming and roots.

Moral and practical uncertainties are parts of business life: where does one make a stand; where does one draw the line between being smart and staying straight? Does business have a history which matters? What part does business play in our civilization, and where is it going? Does business need an ideology? Is liberty important? Readers will not find all their answers here. They may find one or two, or none. But they will at least have considered the questions.

Much has been written on civilization, and much on business. Writers like Simon Schama have given us brilliant descriptions of business civilizations in particular periods.[1] But few if any books have related business in general to civilization in general. This book, then, being a first attempt, opens the subject and invites amendment.

There are three parts.

The first part, The Present, has two sections. Section 1 deals with a businessman's everyday concerns: with leadership, selling, prices, negotiation and taxation. Section 2 widens the scope to examine the relationship between politics, liberty and business.

Part 2, The Past, reviews the origins of the business system. First, in section 3, is a brief examination of commercial history in general, then, in section 4, the unfolding of ideas on the universalities and the morality of money from a businessman's, rather than an academic's, point of view. Two very different 'outsiders', the Jews and their dispersion, the Japanese and their clustered culture, are considered in section 5.

Part 3, The Future, also has two sections. The first, section 6, reflects on the altered definition of business and society in its relation to machine intelligences. The second, section 7, examines the relationship between business and civilization, and concludes the general arguments of the book.

At this or that point in the book the question will inevitably arise whether some arguments and statements refer to what *is*, or to what *should* be. The question shall remain unanswered. Readers must decide the matter for themselves.

Throughout the term 'man' is used to include the term 'woman'. Because of the history of things, including the history of the English language, the equal respect the writer feels for businesswomen cannot be expressed simultaneously in English sentences without great awkwardness.

This writing is not a work of original scholarship and lays no claim to erudition. It claims to be written in the ways a businessman thinks: with an eye to the relevance of even the most abstract problems to business. If this occasionally involves contradiction, then, as much else in business life, so be it.

The writer owes a great debt to his wife, who has accompanied him through approximately a one-hundredth part of the recorded history of business. Four years ago, he owed his introduction to the subject to Miriam Beard, whose *History of the Businessman* was published in 1938,[2] and is now out of print. She dipped her pen into the inkpots of commercial history deeply and elegantly, and her book deserves to be again available.

Many business books were read by the writer, few remembered, before the making of this one. A number of them, published in the last twenty-five years, proved to be ephemeral; many aspired to science but attained neither to this nor to art. The best of them were autobiographical: books that recorded not the facts alone, but the grim trials and rich fruits of business life as well.

When a businessman retires, he rarely finds it possible to do so completely. He does something, not for fame, but, as here, from 'the habit of laboriousness.' From years of business and many dry pages, the writer hopes to have expressed a usable drop to add to the great crock of business.

Notes

1 *The Embarrassment of Riches: Dutch Culture in the Golden Age.* Knopf Inc., New York, and Collins, London, 1987.
2 Miriam Beard, *A History of the Businessman* Macmillan, New York, 1938.

Introduction

What unity does business have, with its persistent and obstinate diversity of aims, an infinity of means for their achievement, a pursuit of divergence and advantage, a knowing or unknowing war against competitors, a search for profitable inequalities, a constant overcoming of intemperate expectations and temptations? What unity is this?

Apart from the essential but trivial unity of uniform accounting, only two other unities: the urge to achieve, and the maintenance of standards.

Of standards there are also two, and both unfashionable: the duty to lead, and the duty to serve – 'duty taught and understood'.

The concept of duty has receded in our day: consumers as economic men are attended to by producers as organization men. This being so, man has been abstracted – man who must outlive these fleshless substitutes. Economic man feels no duty to others, and, assuredly, organization man feels no duty to economic man – the wooing of consumers notwithstanding.

There is a lack of symmetry: states have found no fruitful ways to reciprocate the loyalty of citizens, and corporations have found no fulfilling ways to reciprocate the personal loyalty (where it exists) of their members. If the Western business system has a weakness, this is it, and it has so far not found a settlement.

Of remedies there are also two. One of them is the habit of deliberate smallness. This writer has never found a business which, in human terms, was big. Rigidity, not size, makes business big. Arrogance makes it even bigger. It, and intrigue, may be big business, but both are sure to make it worse. Bigness refers to a corporation's size, not to a corporation's *business*.

But in the end, even big businesses are constellations of small clusters of discernible identity, in cousinship with other clusters of equally discernible identity. What makes a difference is the quality (including the human quality) of the people in each cluster, and the affinity (including familial affinity) they have with those in other clusters. No doubt some men and some clusters spend great sums essential to the corporation. Other men and clusters spend small sums – equally essential to the limbs of the corporation. Clusters originate, not merely execute. It is not easy, in the face of their differences of scale and function, to achieve a condition of equal esteem between the clusters, but it is a better condition for a company than one of feudal ranking.

The other remedy is the habit of deliberate freshness. The sustenance of freshness is a businessman's first duty to himself. The maintenance and encouragement of freshness is the business leader's first duty to his fellow-workers. An absence of freshness turns the present into a barrier against the future, and confines the business mind to fears, preoccupations and passing urgencies.

The preceding is not so much an introduction to the contents of the book as an introduction to its disposition. Like most introductions, it was the last thing to be written.

PART I

Present

Section 1

Attributes of Business

Preamble

We shall look at Western business civilization from three points of view: as history, as an evolution of ideas and from the point of view of two special cultures. But first, in this part, we turn selectively to the present – with civility in business intercourse an underlying theme.

We think in generalities, the philosopher said, but live in detail. Books of the present kind have to generalize because detail would only describe the contents of each man's pockets. Nowhere is this more evident than in this section, which deals with leadership, salesmanship, negotiation and taxation. There are some, but there are few, universal rules of business. Almost every statement one can make about it has exceptions (including, of course, this statement). One has, therefore, to persevere and state the general case.

One theme is leadership. Business leadership is not, ultimately, a matter of money and means. It is a matter of knowledge and above all, of courage. The Japanese, for example, after the Second World War, built factories and conquered markets with great boldness. They had, we now know, the courage to see that Americans had lost much of theirs.

The theme of leadership which follows omits any mention of honesty. It does so for the reason that honesty, while implicit in all business dealings, does not itself derive from business.

Honesty is indeed a dull and awkward subject. On the one hand one knows that a man who is honest, not for fear of hell or to gain heaven, but simply because that is how he is, is a worthy man and admirable. On the other hand one also knows that if the water is too pure, fish won't swim in it.

But one can at least say what honesty is not. Item: it is not the same as respectability; Ivar Kreuger, the Swedish Match King who pyramided many companies until his monopoly collapsed in the greatest financial scandal of 1932 and then committed suicide, was respectable enough to have had the Grand Cross of the French Legion of Honour bestowed on him by France's President Poincaré only two years before he was exposed as a rogue. Item: sincerity has little to do with honesty; Hitler managed to 'sum up the world in a single lie',[1] and quite sincerely murdered millions. Item: the objections to hypocrisy are exaggerated: it does not matter that the man who signs the cheque is a hypocrite; what matters is that the bill is paid. Item: no honesty is complete that does not weigh consequences. To maximize profits for the next few months at the expense of future years is not the pinnacle of honest management. Item: God save us from honest fools. Honesty without well-informed intelligence is half a virtue. For one thing it takes an intelligent man to recognize another's honesty as a strength. Item: Involvement in one's business must not become an all-consuming passion. It will not do to keep one's ear so close to the ground that one cannot hear the words of an upright man.[2] Item: whatever things high rewards may achieve, greater honesty is not always one of them. In some managers the *sacra fames*, the unholy greed for gold, increases as their bonuses increase. Item: whether or not power corrupts, the fear of loss of power corrupts most; desperate businessmen often prove newly capable of turning their fallen hopes into false pretences. Item: common sense eschews dirty deals. Bribery is hard to define, but by its shortest definition, it is buying the sale. The price of such sales is high and will rise with each repetition, and being devious business, waste a lot of time. But then, for those who are prepared to enter into them, 'do as you like – and pay.'[3] In the end, it all depends on what one wants to see in the mirror; oneself, or, instead, a rich man doubtfully.

Finally, complexity blunts morality: if it is too complex, even the truth distorts into a lie. Then again, truth also depends on the manner of its telling. A violin sonata is an encounter between a cat's intestines and a horse's tail – true or false? Not false; not true either.

For corporations, honesty is to be found less in intention than in structure: if the boundaries are defined and the means are straight, so is the business.

One of the moral tightropes of business is the price behaviour which economists sometimes call oligopoly: the universal tendency of corporations not to undercut current market prices in the short run, and thereby drive the market down. This tendency to price congruence is, however, rational and defensible. If it is a conspiracy, it is overwhelmingly one without conspirators.

Businesses that compete with one another are caught in the 'prisoners' dilemma': imagine two prisoners being interrogated separately. If neither confesses, each will have to go to prison for one year. If both confess, each will spend five years in prison. If one turns state's evidence and confesses, he will go free, but the other will receive a ten-year sentence. Should they confess? Or not confess? Businessmen, in choosing price congruity, are like prisoners who choose not to confess – which, if one considers the alternatives, is rational.

Price congruence does not last. It breaks down in the medium run – and so it should. But meanwhile, from profits, it makes accumulation to develop new products, processes and services possible. It is not a perfect but a stable mode of price behaviour.

Peter Drucker is right: inside the firm there are only costs; the profits are outside. The mood inside a corporation is not necessarily the mood of the world in which it finds itself, any more than is the mood in a monastery's cloister the temper of life for the peasants in the fields outside it. A corporation whose managers do not from time to time immerse themselves in the turbulent waters of their market soon forget how to catch fish.

There are some truths of salesmanship which can be listed. Item: the salesman's product is not *what* he sells, but *that* he sells; his product is The Order. Item: the salesman knows and likes his product because one does not sell well without involvement. But he is not in love with it because it makes him insensitive. Item: he does not use every possible argument because he then risks using one argument too many. He prefers to leave a strong impression, and leave. Item: he avoids *ad hominem* arguments – arguments addressed to the buyer's prejudices rather than his business interests. In the end business interests prevail over flattery and puffery. Item: when he sells he does not falsely strain to create a presumption of exclusivity, nor does he pretend to have a monopoly when, anyway, an edge, a one per cent monopoly, will do the job. Item: if possible, he does not just tell his customer, but shows him, because miracles are more persuasive than sermons. Item: he does not assume that a buyer knows less than he does. Having talked to many salesmen, the buyer often knows more. The salesman is always selling, but the buyer is not always buying; he is always learning and comparing. Lastly, he is not misled by large enquiries of doubtful parentage; he considers the source and does not waste his time on the management of myth. But as for myths, the salesman will endure; he will remain the same old Sisyphus, occasionally changing stones but never mountains.

Notes

1 The late banker Siegmund Warburg's phrase.
2 Remark made by J. M. Keynes. Quoted in D. Worswick and James Trevithik (eds), *Keynes and the Modern World*, Cambridge University Press, Cambridge, 1983, p. 265.
3 A Chinese proverb.

I

Personal Attributes in Business

Entrepreneurship and Autonomy

The enduring passion of businessmen is for achievement. Money matters very much to them, but not money alone. Businessmen mind their money, of course, and value it for what it brings, but they also value it as a measuring rod of achievement.

Power matters to them, as it does to all ambitious men, but less than some believe. Few of them are found in politics. If power mattered more to them, they would be there in greater numbers. Which is, perhaps, as well: the corridors of power might become too crowded. The power they have to conduct their business is a sufficient substitute for any other power.

Fame is no great spur to them either, although they want a good reputation among their peers. Most are frightened of fame. Many of them would consider a television interview as terrifying as an appearance in a court of law to hear judgement against them.

Achievement is what they seek. It is a source of pride to them to have gained a growth in sales; or a better balance sheet showing good earnings and good financial ratios; or to have opened a new plant; or to have reduced costs; or to have been given a better rating by the banks; or to have managed deeper market penetration; or to have made better products. Achievement is the spur. If more money and more power attend achievement, so much the better, they say; accumulation will enable them to start into more fulfilments.

One can overstate the point. They certainly 'ask that Fortune send / a little more than I shall spend'. But their complaints are muted if Fortune sends them no more than this modest dividend.

They often evoke the image of coldly reasoned self-interest, and there are, undeniably, cold men among them. But because businessmen have to take risks, and because reason alone cannot take them into certainty, there is always a vision behind the risk that spurs them on; they are often passionate dreamers who are prepared, sometimes, to grow thorns for the sake of the roses. Their vision, and perhaps their pride, is sometimes taken to the point of enthusiasm for perfection, rather than for good sense and good profits.

The scoundrels among them excepted, businessmen's passion is also a patient passion, because they know that their harvests will often be long in coming. But it is passion using reason as its slave, not master.

Contrary to belief, businessmen are not concerned merely to satisfy the market. They try as hard to dissatisfy as to satisfy. They are rarely to be believed when they pay lip service to the satisfaction of the market. When they launch the new product they want to displace the old product – their own old product or their competitor's new and old product. The fashion industry cannot abide the hemline of the previous year.

Judged by social convention, most businessmen are not gentlemen, and mostly none the worse for it. If gentlemanliness is to live a certain rarefied style of life, they forgo the privilege; it would lead them away from business into another world. But if a gentleman is one to whom money may be a necessity but is not a temptation, there are some gentlemen among them.

They are ambitious. Ambition, depending on the means it employs, is either a term of praise or a condemnation. But ambition in the exercise of wealth is generally more benign than ambition in the exercise of political power. Undeniably there are many businessmen of boundless and ruthless ambition. With some notable exceptions, however, their fortunes, acquired rapidly and ruthlessly, do not outlast the next economic rip tide.

Some of them seek security. Now, a sense of security is in the mind. Real security may be, and may not be, an illusion. Security is certainly not the same as regularity, with which many confuse it. The fact that salary payments arrive punctually every month, and have done so for years, is no guarantee that fate will not overtake an industry or corporation, and them with it.

Just as many of them are ambitious, so many of them are conceited, because conceit is a parent of ambition. But achievement in business is real and measurable; profit-and-loss statements measure performance. Nor can conceit overcome competition. So, while some of them are ambitious and some of them conceited, they are always reined in by facts and forced to sobermindedness. Those whom success has made conceited had best remember that if they believe that they deserve all that they have gained, they must also accept that they will deserve all that they may lose.

They live with risk, a habit which starts as a gnawing disquiet and ends by becoming part of the normal daily challenge. They become used to it. They even miss it when, on rare occasions, it is absent. Anxiety is for them, as it is for actors about to go onstage, a daily and familiar drug.

But risk does not make them gamblers. They try to make their choices thoughtfully – unlike the gentleman who knew nothing about chicken farming, but bought a chicken farm on the theory that the chickens knew. Still, they make mistakes. Fate and luck still matter, and it is unfortunately true that 'all business is a bet,' that 'even honesty is a financial speculation,' but that, to balance matters out, 'fortune comes to the prepared mind.'

Their faults are glaring. They have a fatal inclination to give themselves up to false hope, their great enemy. Businessmen are, as we said, creatures of passion long before they are creatures of reason. Excessive hopefulness is like calenture, a delusion known to sailors in the tropics long ago. They thought they saw green pastures, 'enamelled fields and verdant trees', where there were only green waves. They leaped down to walk on grass and drowned. The Russian novelist Turgenev once warned that any prayer is a request for God to grant that twice two be not four. And yet hopefulness may be their most indispensable virtue. They cannot work without its light. But as it becomes a vice, it often breaks them.

We know as witnesses that more business failures are due to overtrading, overextension, overexpansion, too many hopes, than have ever been caused by economic recessions. We are late in drawing this conclusion: Daniel Defoe, author of *Robinson Crusoe* and himself a merchant, said it in 1732: 'It is an observation indeed of my own, but I believe . . . that there are more Tradesmen undone by having too much trade, than for want of trade.'[1]

More trouble is caused by exaggerated expectations than by too modest fulfilments. Expanding a business is not the most difficult art. The most difficult art is knowing how to rein in when the pointers of the times say that we must. The general inclination is to continue, and to hope for better times, whereas experiences says that better times may come too late for waiting. When the gross profit is a million, an overhead cost of half a million is modest; but when profits more than halve, it becomes an invitation to disaster. To learn when to say no is an art, greater perhaps than the art of saying yes. The best art is knowing when to stop.

Nonetheless, hopefulness as a virtue is better than hopefulness as a vice. It is not possible to run a business without good expectations. Business disasters due to excessive hopefulness are like the relationship between traffic and accidents: without traffic there would be no accidents – and no traffic either. Some hopefulness is necessary, but on the other hand, the idea of enduring management based on hope is as absurd as the idea of a god praying to himself.

The businessman's worst faults are the sins of omission. There is the inertia of routine; too much untempered self-confidence; delegation of what should be his own duty; failure to delegate what should be the duty of others; hasty analysis; laziness; not passing information; putting off to tomorrow what should be done today; assuming that time will cure what his actions have not cured; not pursuing opportunity and being blind to opportunity. Such is the 'long defeat of doing nothing well'.

There is, finally, his constant lazy inclination to let the urgent displace the important; to cosset his beloved and familiar headaches; to busy himself with the leak and not the dyke. An eighteenth-century French wit said that the lazy are always wanting to do something, and an English wit of the same period said that there is no kind of idleness by which we are as easily seduced as that which dignifies itself by the appearance of business.

Leaks must be mended but to live with a finger in the dyke is unhelpful to construction. The businessman might recall that the Greeks first distinguished between urgency and importance, and that this was their greatest invention. Until then, few had spent much time on such nonurgent matters as the nature of man; the nature of beauty, of good and of evil; the nature of nature and of numbers. And yet the first led to theories and practices of statecraft; the second to ethics and theology; the third to mathematics and the sciences.

Urgencies pass and other urgencies arise, but it simply will not do to bring the future to a table bare of everything except the crumbs of long-forgotten urgencies.

Leadership and Management

Good leadership can be sensed but not defined. Certainly, a good leader is one who has the gift of 'automatic competence'. And a good leader is one who knows what to do when expediency is at odds with principle.

But styles of leadership are diverse, and so is the advice given. The great Blaise Pascal (1623–62), in his *Pensées*, says that the servant does not know what his master is about, because the master tells him only what to do and not the purpose, and this is why he obeys slavishly and often frustrates the purpose.

Disagreeing, the late Dag Hammarskjöld, Secretary-General of the United Nations, in *Markings*, wants us to tell others only what is of importance to them; to ask them only what one needs to know; to limit the conversation to what the speaker really possesses; to argue only to reach a conclusion; to think aloud only with those to whom this means something. Pascal called for open leadership, Hammarskjöld did not.

Leaders are either intellectual or intuitive or aristocratic. By 'aristocratic' one does not mean persons of ancient lineage. One means men chosen to lead because they are craggy-faced, impassive chairmen, named when the board was unable to agree on any other leader. One dismisses them for the same reason that made the captaincy of the *Titanic* a temporary appointment.

Intellectual leaders cut a swath of practical solutions through thickets of complexity. Intuitive leaders, on the other hand, do not attempt to integrate complexity; they sense their way to a solution. They are often found among statesmen and politicians.

One may admire the first kind more than the second kind. But, given problems with a high enough level of abstraction and generality – problems of consequence and prophecy too complex for mere logic – it is not easy to distinguish the intellectual from the intuitive leader. Style then becomes more important than analysis. It made great statesmen of men like Winston Churchill, whose attainment at school was undistinguished.

The greatest of them can see a possible reality and make it happen. Charles de Gaulle was of that kind, so was a late acquaintance, Konrad Adenauer. Their leadership was not by words alone, which they often used with great simplicity. Churchill, too, was of that company. He had the courage to speak slowly. One of his obituaries said that his words had the quality of deeds. There is a wordlessness beyond speech about great leadership.

Great merchants and entrepreneurs, however outwardly various, generally have four characteristics in common. First, they tend to be at heart simple, though not necessarily modest, which is to say that they have strong innate moral criteria. Second, they judge a current transaction in the light of their perspective of the future. They do not waste time 'churning the void in the hope of making butter'.[2] Third, they define their own standards and do not live by received wisdoms. Fourth, they have great self-awareness. Knowing complexity, they also know simplicity. Though their decisions at first may seem oblique, they may also prove ultimately apt.

Whatever the nature of their greatness, such men see reality differently. It was true of those mentioned; it was also true of great scientists – Galileo, Newton, Darwin, Freud, Einstein. Their vision was not obvious until they made us look at the world anew. They were often stubborn men and unreasonable with others. George Bernard Shaw saw that reasonable men adapt themselves to the world, but that unreasonable men persist in trying to adapt the world to themselves, and that, therefore, all progress depends on unreasonable men. This may not be entirely true, but makes the point. Progress depends on the greatness of the vision. It also depends on deep immersion in a problem.

Except perhaps in the demand for junior officers in times of war, the demand for leaders is greater in business than in any other walk of life. In most areas of human endeavour we can stand on the shoulders of the giants of the past. Only one Newton or Einstein is needed to discover a law of nature. One man can make an epoch in art, music, and architecture. In politics one man can strike an enduring note which defines his nation's course for many years.

But not in business: we cannot stand on the shoulders of giants. Time shrinks our giants. We need an endless supply of them. To a statement that the writers of the past are remote from us because we know so much more than they did, T. S. Eliot replied that *they* are precisely what we know. He meant that art coming from the past is not superseded; it stands alongside the art of later ages.

But business, for all that it has a past, is not remembered for it. In business, unlike art, the past is physically and financially, and in other ways, depreciated in the books. In the opinion of Miriam Beard, a chronicler of business through the ages,[3] the businessman struggles on, unfathered and unhallowed, lacking annals and allegories. He is his own ancestor.

The businessman's past is cast away. To business, apart from a valuable spirit of good tradition (where it exists), and apart from obsolescent technical legacies, history *is* bunk. For all practical purposes it only has its present fighting for its future. And if Henry Ford's saying is true, then, so far as Ford Motors is concerned today, Henry Ford is also bunk. And so every opening for a new chief executive is a cry for a genius to take a corporation from now into its future. In management, the time for the first act of creation is always today. However great a departing chief may have been, we need a greater one – immediately.

One must try to find chief executives of the highest possible quality, because a brilliant leader is likely to want to hire brilliant assistants. To this statement there are exceptions: brilliant prima donnas – comets that come, then vanish. On the other hand, it is almost certain that a dull leader will not recruit brilliant rivals.

Enterprise and Wisdom

However wise he may be, no man's judgement is infallible. But what is wisdom? Like the idea of time, we know it, yet we don't. One turns to Francis Bacon, who said much that is wise, and to Erasmus of Rotterdam, who talked wisely about folly, but finds no definition. So, being unable to define wisdom, one must copy what Bacon might have said of it, but did not say: Wisdom is a shrewd serenity of judgment, but wisdom is not unalloyed virtue. It bows its head before power if the times so require, but it makes no pact with the devil. Wisdom loves Honesty, but has her for a secret lover. Wisdom chooses, if need be, to live in tents but is ever ready to build in stone. Wisdom does not cast its eyes up to heaven; it ponders earthly things. It knows what works and what does not: it never pretends that all the ways to good are straight and noble roads. It looks to the future but is rarely found in the casinos of prophecy. Wisdom is neither virgin nor whore; it is prudent but not pure; is canny but not humble. But wisdom is not hypocritical and knows its own retreats; neither does it descend to common cunning, because 'we take cunning for a sinister and crooked wisdom.'[4]

We do not know what wisdom is, but we know that wisdom is a deep understanding of the relative value of things. We also know that men who lack wisdom often have wide knowledge but narrow feelings.

When is it wise for a man to start his own business? There is a decade in every man's life – and there is always such a decade – when business friendships, connections, knowledge, energy, experience and reputation flow together. It is the decade when he must add pertinacity and courage to the list.

If he starts his own business in his twenties, it is mainly from exuberance. If in his thirties, it is mainly from energy. If in his forties, it is mainly from experience. If in his fifties, it is mainly from necessity. If in his sixties, it is mainly too late. An early, but not too early start, is best. When young, failure is a setback from which one can recover: the safety net is spread of useful decades still to come. If he fails, he has time to start again – employed or self-employed. There is no safety net for him after fifty. But

> There was never any more inception than there is now,
> Nor any more youth or age than there is now;
> And will never be any more perfection than there is now,
> Nor any more heaven or hell than there is now.[5]

And if he decides to start his own business, these principles are to be observed in the conduct of a corporation: build on strength and not from scratch. Reinforce success, not failure. Stay within the limits of the possible. Remember that growth transforms that which grows.

Judgement and the Making of Decisions

When newly in business, one is ready to submit to the judgement of one's seniors, though of a different judgement oneself. Since it is their money and one is paid by them, one does as told, and that is right. Much later, when oneself in charge, one can apply the judgements of one's younger days – and find that they can turn out well.

To acquire knowledge is the first stepping stone. Any market has its own usages and culture, and is animated by its own rationale. The number of people who constitute any single market is small – it is a

PERSONAL ATTRIBUTES IN BUSINESS

club of sorts. Suppliers and customers are members, so are competitors. And while one must contend against competitors, they share in that unity of knowledge which is what we call a market. When we have become part of the gossip of the market place, we have become established in it.

The second step is to derive judgement from knowledge: the Japanese, before they make a decision, make a detailed inventory of the present. It is their way of saying that even a good army moves on its belly. If one first learns to know exactly where one stands, the compass will point, not necessarily in the right direction, but away from the wrong one. In other words, direction begins from location.

The next step is trust in our judgement: making a decision never came easily to any businessman. It is not so much the possible consequences which make one uncertain; with crystal-clear vision and knowledge of circumstances, decisions are easy. The agony is only there when the vision is blurred, and the consequences several. Making decisions is a burden when so much and so many are involved and must be borne alone. But as the years roll on, the burden lightens by acquaintance.

Some have no problems with decisions. 'This court,' a judge once said, 'may sometimes be in error; but it is never in doubt.' Which may be possible for judges, whose errors are confined, but is not at all simple for those of us in business.

And then there are the decisions that seem small at the time, but turn out to be fateful far beyond their innocent appearance. It is easier to judge the quality of effects than their scale. Confidence is needed, and confidence is infectious. One must learn to firmly trust oneself; it is a sad leader who struggles to be strong.

Last, despite the risks, comes acting on one's judgement. Mistakes are a genuine and necessary business cost, and inaction from fear of mistakes is worse than most mistakes. Mistakes teach unforgettably. A German business friend, senior and shrewd, was in the habit of rehearsing his train of thought aloud – facts, deductions, possible decisions. Then, suddenly, he would say '*Halt, Denkfehler!*' – 'stop, faulty reasoning'. He would then retrace and correct his train of thought. It is good to mumble to oneself or to a trusted friend. Another, the Managing Director of a British company many years ago, when proudly shown all the orders a young man who worked for him had invoiced in the previous month, only remarked: 'You made a profit on each one. No losses. You can't have been trying hard enough. If you had, you would have made *some* losses.'

Business does not deal in great profundities. It is a profession with no settled philosophy of its own. Businesspeople weigh what happens to others without demur – as long as it does not touch their own business. They are for regulation when it is good for them; they are against it when it is bad for them or, if good, too expensive. In other words, they accept most things – for others.

But businessmen must not be taken to the ultimate test of moral choice: whether they will, in times of crisis, self-sacrificially uphold an ultimate good, even though this might lead them to self-destruction. They are not martyrs. They may, when *in extremis*, watch their neighbour being thrown to the wolves – if this is the price of their own survival. In this, they are not alone. Stock exchanges and financial markets are established on the same principle: my gain may be your loss, and my loss your gain – and I don't know you.

But every business has a fund of tiny wisdoms on which it builds its empires. One of the small truths to guide one young man's conduct was given to him many years ago by a now long-retired corporation president in Alabama. Play it smart and play it straight, he said.

It used to be said that one cannot be both wise and rich. It is no longer true.

Notes

1 Daniel Defoe, *The Complete English Tradesman*, 3rd edn. 1732, p. 57.
2 Justice Oliver Wendell Holmes.
3 Miriam Beard, *A History of the Businessman*, Macmillan, New York, 1938, p. 1.
4 The last nine words are, in fact, Francis Bacon's own. *Essays* XXII.
5 Walt Whitman, *Leaves of Grass*.

2

Value Attributes in Enterprise

Price and Value

Those of us who have a certain respect for the market system and for its great advocate Adam Smith, author of *The Wealth of Nations* more than two centuries ago, may be surprised that it was he, not Marx or Lenin, who said that civil government was instituted to uphold the rich against the poor, and that the wealth of the few rested on the poverty of the many. It was he who spoke about a 'nation of shopkeepers' and the 'mean rapacity' of merchants who are not permitted now, and ought never be permitted to rule. It was he, and not some red-toothed, wild-eyed revolutionary, who said that wherever merchants meet they contrive a conspiracy against the public to raise prices. Which gets us to the point.

There are many prices, and many age-old debates about them. There are natural or prime prices based on cost, and just prices based on equity; prices and values in use (like the high value of a glass of water to a thirsty man) and prices and values in exchange (like the low value of a glass of water from the kitchen tap). There are market prices, oligopoly prices, monopoly prices. There are dumping prices, loss-leader prices, full-cost prices, incremental prices, 'creaming' prices for new products, government-subsidized prices. There are export prices and domestic prices. The list is certain to be incomplete, but somewhere, floating in the air beyond the target, is the right price.

Debate has been, and will continue to be, unending: political, technical, economic, historical, philosophical, theological debate.

Political debate: is a socialist system better or worse than a system in which prices are set by a free market, and if so, where is the dividing line?

Technical debate: what correlation is there between price, profit, volume and market share?

Economic debate: is free trade to be admitted even if it means that low-cost foreign exports can destroy high-cost domestic industries and put people out of work?

Historical debate: did mercantilism, protectionism and colonialism do some good at some stages of history although they raised prices or exploited peoples?

Philosophical and theological debates: has price anything to do with justice? Is a living mouse more valuable than dead wheat? And if so, as seen by whom? By God or citizens or merchants?

All these debates assume, overtly or covertly, that businessmen try to increase their profits unjustly – at the expense of the public. This is true in some cases, but false in most. In most cases, the paramount object of price policy is that volume of sales, and that price stability, which will ensure a proper return on investment. A return, namely, which makes it worthwhile to keep shop, manufacture, stock and trade, rather than put the money into savings, shares, bonds or hoards.

Unfortunately this plain fact does not solve the problem – the problem being this: seen from the point of view of the supplier, price is a matter of a morally neutral fair return. From the point of view of the public, and sometimes of government, it is a matter of fairness and justice. Fairness and justice are highly charged with emotion.

How can it be otherwise, since price is the consideration payable for value received, and while price is in the purse, value is in the mind. Price is a hard but value a soft estimate; price sparkles, but the glow of value is diffused. The market provides the price, but, except in driest economic theory, not all the satisfactions.

But see it reverse. Justice apart, as seen by the buyer, price is a simple thing. The figure on the ticket is clear cut and comparisons between one supplier and another are quantitatively easy. But as seen by the supplier, price is a tangled web; it is the mean of all considerations. In the case of new products or new markets, it is also the mean of all anticipations.

Plainly a distinction must be made between fact and opinion. Opinions, such as what has value, may be argued – but not facts. There is something singular about price. Price, uniquely, is the attempt to join value with reality. Not any value, of course, and not all values; the measure of such things as life, liberty, loyalty or beauty is inaccessible to price. But justice is accessible, and if not full justice, then at least just rents and prices.

And so, price is a scale for the value of things for which there is no other measure. It is to an economy what justice is to the law: related but not identical.

The Architecture of Price

Behind the price, that basic brick, lies an architecture of value. It is the architecture of the market system, of that gigantic sorting mechanism which is capitalism. It does not allocate compassion, justice or brotherly love, but it allocates resources. The most attentive readers of the price lists of Western companies and the keenest collectors of information on Western market prices are the planners of the Eastern Bloc who have few other means of reference – even to the prices of their own products. One (rare) mention of price in an authoritative Marxist book on planning says that in purely socialist economies, as in the Soviet Union, part of the national income is retained by the State through selling consumers' goods at prices higher than their cost of production. And if not that, then at subsidised prices.[1] The result of all this central planning is that a Russian-made car in Russia costs between six and eight times its price in Iceland.

For all its imperfections, the habit of competition is the most productive habit under which an economy can grow and prosper. One shop is monopoly; two shops are competition; three shops are a market, it is said. It is also said that there are no export markets – only several home markets. If competition does nothing else for international understanding, at least the prices it sets are one form of communication between them; they add comparability to the traffic between nations, and sometimes give them discipline.

As a shrewd Japanese observer remarked, when one tries to achieve or maintain a position of relative superiority over competitors, the mind functions very differently from the way it does when the object is to make routine internal improvements: 'It is the difference between going into battle and going on a diet.'[2]

Notes

1 Oskar Lange, *Essays on Economic Planning*, Statistical Publishing Society, Calcutta, 1960.
2 Kenichi Ohmae, *The Mind of the Strategist*, McGraw-Hill, New York, 1982.

3

Attributes of Marketing

Legends of Salesmanship

There are stories, real and invented, of salesmen with the courage of Achilles and the cunning of Ulysses. There was, for example, a motorist who stopped at a lonely one-pump station in the wilds of Texas to buy a replacement tyre, with little hope of obtaining it in such a desolate place. But the station's owner showed him a very large barn filled to the rafters with tyres. The motorist expressed his surprise that a small station in the middle of nowhere was able to sell so many tyres. The owner explained that he could himself sell very few, but that the salesman who had sold him the tyres could sell many.

Another is to be found in the history preceding the amalgamation of Cecil Rhodes's and Rothschild's interests into De Beers Consolidated Mines of South Africa. A third name in the amalgamation was Barney Barnato, the younger son of a London East-End dealer who went out to the Cape in 1873 at the age of 20, and steadily accumulated capital by buying and selling diamonds. 'It is said that his first break came when he bought an old nag from a seasoned dealer and allowed the horse to make its own way round the dealer's select clientele.'[1]

Heinemann, the European publisher, tells another story. He noticed two street vendors standing side by side, selling toy dolls. One of them had a queer, fat-faced doll, which he was pushing into the faces of the passers-by, giving it the name of a well-known woman reformer. His dolls were selling rapidly. The man beside him, who really had the more attractive dolls was doing badly.

A thought occurred to Heinemann. He called the second pedlar to one side. 'My friend,' he said, 'do you want to know how to sell twice as many of these dolls as you are selling now? Hold them up in pairs, two together in each hand, and call them "The Heavenly Twins".' It was 1893, a time when a novel of that title by Sarah Grand, attacking sexual double standards and the dangers of venereal disease, enjoyed a high degree of fame.

The vendor somewhat grudgingly followed Heinemann's advice. The Heavenly Twins dolls were an immediate success. Within an hour the other vendor gave up the fight, acknowledged himself beaten, and moved down the street to escape the competition. The relationship between the book and the dolls was, of course, wholly illogical, but it succeeded just the same.[2]

A story, supposedly true, used to be told about another South African company. A cousin of the celebrated Sir Ernest Oppenheimer – one of the richest men of his day and founder of The Diamond Corporation – was a dealer in agricultural supplies in South Africa when the Boer War broke out at the turn of the century. This cousin gambled on the fact that some regiments of horse about to be sent from the United Kingdom would arrive in the southern hemisphere in the false belief that fresh hay was available there in winter – it being summer in Britain at the time. Cousin Oppenheimer chartered one or two large ships to bring redolent hay from the lush pampas of the Argentine, to coincide with the arrival of the regimental horses in South Africa. Just when the Army Ordnance of Britain faced the fact that horses without fodder would not make an effective cavalry, cousin Oppenheimer found himself in possession both of hay and its monopoly. His gamble turned out to have been correct. According to our informant, the unhappiness of the British War Office at having to pay too much for fodder was not shared by cousin Oppenheimer.

The name Oppenheimer brings to mind a definition by a nineteenth-century Frankfurt goldsmith called Oppenheim: 'Selling a pearl you own to someone who wants to buy it is not selling. But selling a pearl you do not own to someone who does not want it – that is selling.' The remark is witty, and witty is all it is.

Some forty years ago, a gullible and inexperienced young salesman was ready to believe stories of powerful salesmanship. He was then the steel-pipe trader at a London merchant company. Having brought and sold pipe made by several European manufacturers with reasonable success, he wrote a letter to one from whom he had tried to buy some of his supplies but had not succeeded because of this manufacturer's high prices. In it, he expressed the hope that the manufacturer would bring his prices down to the level of other manufacturers so that they could do business together. The reply – long, polite and patronizing – said approximately this: to sell cheaply needed only a dog for salesman, to be sent into the streets with a printed placard attached to its tail, reading 'Our Prices Are The Lowest'; the true art of selling was to overcome the hurdle of price by greater arts. It was a humbling letter to a young man from an older and wiser man.

The young man continued to sell, more or less satisfactorily, at the lowest price and on the best conditions possible, because he could find no satisfactory arts to make his pipe, which was fit for all plumbers, fit for rich plumbers only. He regrets that the corporation whose sales manager had sent him the letter went out of business some years later for want of competitiveness. A policy involving the dog would, ultimately, have served them better.

The myth of the brilliant salesman obscures the truth. The consummated sale is only one stage in a continuum; it is neither the first nor the last stage. The single sale – The Deal – rarely makes enough money for survival over the years, any more than an expensive machine tool can when used only once to make a single part.

International trade, too, is trade in which the customer is often neither seen nor personally known. But international trade is selling all the same, with readiness to stand by the product and the promise, with reputation, preparation, knowledge, and reliability all involved. Charm and fine words are no substitute for these; only those succeed in it who understand their business well enough to 'know the dollars by their names'.

But given the rest, neither are charm and salesmanship a hindrance. There is pleasure in seeing agreeable, competent, helpful and honest advocates for their company. Customer fidelity to a product and its supplier is generally greater when a good salesman is the symbol for it. There is, as yet, no adequate substitute for the confidence of one man in another, and none is likely. Machines cannot negotiate the negotiable. One cannot shake hands with advertisements. Only a salesman can sense trouble or opportunity, and can prevent an old customer relationship from waning. He is the outpost at the borders between buying and selling companies. In this role, there is no device to supersede him which is both sensitive and subtle.

Salesmen – Born or Made

The often-asked question whether salesmen are made or born is a red herring. The argument is, in a sense, not unlike the different views concerning the nature of man held by the late seventeenth-century Englishman, Locke, and the early seventeenth-century Frenchman, Descartes.

Locke, like Aristotle before him, believed that man is born stripped of all ideas and has to acquire them by experience – which may be stretched to mean that salesman are made. Descartes, on the other hand, believed that men are born ready clothed in innate ideas – which may be stretched to mean that men are born with the talent of instinctive salesmanship. One may incline to Locke, because salesmanship is hardly likely to be an innate idea. But there is a touch of Descartes in it, since native charmlessness is a poor characteristic for an intending salesman.

The diverse character and diverse styles of salesmanship show that salesmen are not one species, none, at least, that is predictively recognizable – some are flamboyant, others quiet. What all good salesman have in common is an ability to read the minds of buyers; a sense of challenge; and an ability to sense the truth even though it may be hidden behind words of other meanings.

A recital of criteria for the selection of salesmen is tedious. Had Francis Bacon written on the matter in the early seventeenth century, he might perhaps – a few words being indeed by Bacon – have expressed it less tediously: Exclude a zealot from consideration because zealotry is blind; an unfeeling man because he cannot estimate the buyer's needs; an amoral man because he knoweth not the meaning of fair consideration; a fool because he is a fool; a greedy man because greed is short-sighted; a cunning man because cunning is a trick that worketh only once; a phantastical man because he doth not distinguish fact from fancy; a cynical man because cynicism soon sheweth as helpless hate; a narrow rigid man because he cannot tell the vessel from its contents. Choose such a man as feeleth challenge in encounters; whose understanding trembleth with their moods; as discerneth opportunity from rote; such a man as hath a sense for the ripeness of things; as by effort knoweth what he offereth for sale, and his advantage over others; as is neither too humble nor too proud; as is neither too shy nor too bold; one who understandeth that he selleth not himself; who is a courteous ambassador; who is like to that that is committed to him, and reporteth back faithfully; who resteth only when he hath worked all men of weighty opinion on the buying of his wares; who doth not fear to ask; neither pretendeth to know when he doth not know, but learneth; who knoweth the uses of time; a man whose face breedeth regard.

Hot air is not much of a product. Salesmen talk too much. It is their most frequent fault. Not listening comes next.

It is better to converse by a well-timed exchange of silences than too much speech, because many simple and important meanings may drown in a sea of words. They grate, these salesmen whose 'religion is to make a noise'. At least an exchange of silences is an exchange of sorts, and at least silences digest earlier thoughts and do not blur their meaning.

Their other common fault is the failure to ask substantive questions for fear of hearing an adverse answer. Instead, the uncertain salesman procrastinates with busy, strained, ingratiating talk. And so there follows a dreary round of themelessness and variations, at which he expounds, explains and talks; expands, exposits and talks; amplifies, clarifies and talks; comments, interprets and talks; reminisces, glosses and talks; gossips, guesses and talks; while the buyer half-listens and nods his head in disagreement.

He must ask for the order when the time is ripe. It is not only necessary, but courteous. Fortune may smile, and the buyer may offer the order unasked. But not often. Buyers, like maidens, though neither be coy, like to be suitored.

Salesmen are often told not to forget to ask. They rarely forget. They are, however, often afraid to put the question, afraid that the customer may deny them the order, or – can it be? – afraid that the customer may *give* them an order. (The Germans say the 'customer threatens with an order'.) This is especially so when the salesman does not yet really know his own company, pretends he does, and feels a little insecure on what it may be safe to sell, and what will follow. It is also so when his corporation has not provided him with cooperative and willing back-up services. And then, the customer wants to vary payment terms a little, which means a battle with the Treasury Department. He also wants a nipple on his widget, which means a battle with Production. He wants delivery with hitherto unheard-of timeliness, which means a difficult session with Dispatch. Now comes the inside selling to these three other parties who are not inclined to courtesy, and who 'along the cool sequestered vale of life, [just want to keep] the noiseless tenor of their ways'.

A reluctance to ask questions is all the more extraordinary since people are generally pleased to give answers, and feel flattered to be asked. They will rarely think any the worse of the questioner. An intelligent and relevant question speaks for us, not against us.

Understandably, on some occasions we are denied answers. Which is in itself an answer, and better than a question dangling in the air and never put. And sometimes, having asked the question, but having received an honest 'no' for answer instead of an insincere 'call again next week', withdraw with dignity:

> There comes an hour when begging stops,
> When the long interceding lips
> Perceive their prayer is vain.
> 'Thou shalt not' is a kinder sword
> Than from a disappointing god
> 'Disciple, call again.'[3]

But no good man mourns. 'No' would not occur if it were not that 'yes' occurs.

The Art of Negotiation

Businessmen like to be thought of as doers. Most of the time they are talkers. Some of the time they are thinkers. A few of them are listeners. At negotiations all these talents are engaged, particularly the last two. They must also be actors, because even sober negotiation is at heart a drama.

Some attitudes have to be unlearnt. Arrogance, for one, for another, cunning. There are few things in negotiation that annoy a morally straightforward adversary more than a display of flatulent virtuosity with words. Again, great demonstrations of technical professionalism are only proof of narrow learning. They are, in Cicero's phrase, knowledge divorced from any sense of justice. On the other hand, what helps in negotiations is a good reputation, a 'face that breedeth regard', the wisdom of restraint, the habit of good manners.

Above all, long negotiations distinguish the genuinely reasonable man from the fundamentally unreasonable man. The reasonable man will seem increasingly moderate and rational the longer the negotiation, and gain respect. The unreasonable man will begin to seem increasingly irrational and immoderate, and lose respect.

Irrationality does not lie in that certain inclination to private mysticism in matters of the spirit and religion to which even hard-nosed businessmen are often given. Irrationality in business has nothing to do with these private things. In negotiations, irrationality is an inability to sense intuitively and to accept the gradual unveiling of the inevitable in the course of negotiation, and to adapt one's negotiating stance to it in time. Lee Iacocca mentioned two things which do not show themselves in one short job interview: whether a man is lazy, and whether he has any horse sense. In negotiations both reveal themselves.

Negotiation is a rational procedure. Rationality is not necessarily a part of a buyer's or a seller's motives, particularly when it comes to the purchase or sale of his own business. But *understanding* these motives is part of rationality. A friend, a corporate mergers-and-acquisitions expert for many years, was asked how the price for companies was really decided. What were the material factors in the mathematics of valuation? Which factors weigh most in the making of the price? It was much simpler than people seemed to think, he said. No, it was not a multiple of previous years' earnings alone, nor price-to-earnings ratios alone, nor the true market price of understated assets alone, nor unutilized reserves alone, nor even any combination of these factors – alone. What mattered most was what the buyer (or seller) wanted from life. These things are rarely spoken of in negotiations, but may explain why the owners of popular newspaper chains bought the London *Times* or the *Washington Post*. For respectability, perhaps, perhaps from respect.

Consider the export achievements of the Japanese. They are not better individual negotiators than any others. Why then has their international marketing been successful? It is because Japan is a society of civil compromise, a society that has negotiated with itself for centuries and has established the limits of the negotiable. They have observed how Westerners negotiate, and they have found no common treasury of tried approaches there. They found that Western negotiators mostly work not from collective but from individual talent. They found that when the hurdle seemed too high to jump, Westerners were prepared to settle for a lower hurdle.

There are many meetings and discussions when buying from Japan, many courteous dinners and much talk, but remarkably little give-and-take. The concessions with which discussions start are usually the concessions with which they end. They have no need of more because, by the time negotiations start, the Japanese have assessed the probable acceptability of their conditions with great care. For major Japanese corporations as for Emily Dickinson, 'the table is not laid without till it is laid within,' and everything has been done from the very beginning to reduce the need for subsequent concessions.

An example illustrates: to eliminate export competition with other Japanese manufacturers in the steel business, an elaborately run and meticulously recorded 'channelling' system was devised. Customers were assigned to one or other manufacturer through a preferred or nominated exporting corporation. In US terms, it was a method in restraint of competition and assured monopoly. But it worked, if never perfectly, then sufficiently well to have been retained. It left little to negotiations. In the case of major overseas orders each Japanese steel mill shared a part of it with the others. They fought each other – very hard – only for new, as yet unchannelled customers. Korean competition, the rise in the value of the yen, and a general excess of capacity may now be changing all this.

The digression illustrates a point: implied negotiation starts well before face-to-face negotiation. From personal experience, before placing orders, one analyses and asks who has the lowest cost for a particular size; who happens to have a current production run of the same size; who has the greatest need to utilize available manufacturing capacity. Unless the analysis is wrong, (as, of course, it sometimes is), the chosen maker is likely to be interested. Implied negotiation precedes negotiation, and there is usually no need for much additional bargaining: for one per cent perhaps. Now there is only need for loyalty.

Some thirty-five years ago, in Yugoslavia, a young buyer sat at a table facing five men, negotiating at 6.30 in the morning, as was usual then. By local custom, Turkish coffee and plum brandy were served, despite the early hour. One old man had been educated before the First World War, with French as his second language; two, of middle age, with German, from between the Wars; the two young ones had been taught English, since World War II. The buyer had to repeat everything three times: briefly in passable French, briefly in middling

German, briefly in simple English. It did not matter; it encouraged brevity and worked. All spoke the same language.

A business for sale is usually on the brink of change. Few companies, though they were bought with careful purpose, continue to serve that purpose for long without major changes of pattern. This does not argue against negotiations for the purchase of established companies; it argues that what is 'established' is not established for long.

Neither does the value of existing management last for long after the purchase. When a company is for sale, one of the reasons may well be that its managers are weary. It is then best to let them go, with decency. It is better, on the whole, to have managers who are vigorous but have much to learn than to have managers who are experienced but stale. Stale managers do not notice that history moves faster in business than in ordinary life. A year in the fate of corporations is equal to five or more in the fate of nations.

Managers matter as much as good actors in a play. But an indispensable individual is rare, and the more 'indispensable' he is, the sooner he will in fact (and the sooner he must by definition) be replaced. Great men leave an imprint on their corporation. But one must not make too much of it – it vanishes. Salesmen and managers sometimes flatter themselves that their corporation's achievement was wholly theirs – which is a bubble of conceit soon pricked by facts.

One must be wary of 'immortals'. The gods who create are often the same gods who destroy. Henry Ford established the Ford Motor Company in 1908, and nearly broke it in the late twenties. Will Durant, also in 1908, formed the General Motors Company. Two years later, he had it nearly bankrupt. Though he regained his position (by now in the General Motors Corporation), he was never without the supervision, first of banks, then of Pierre du Pont and John Raskob. In 1920 Durant was finally forced to resign.

Be ready to be a little formal, polite, and equable; ready to laugh when tension needs relieving; ready, without rancour, to be softly passionate when your convictions are involved; ready to let passion wane when facts are involved. Speak with economy and do not neglect the opportunity to be silent: silence is a voice which is heard without offence. Do not debate the obvious: what is beyond doubt need not be bargained for.

Look for the sacrificial lambs the adversary may have added and is able to forgo when pressed. Remind yourself of your own irreducible conditions. Then remind yourself of sacrificial lambs that you, too, have added and are prepared to sacrifice when pressed. When you offer them, do not concede with ill humour, but with self-dismissive liberality. Recall what Benjamin Disraeli, who created that once greatest of all multinational corporations, the British Empire, said: 'Next to knowing when to seize an opportunity, the most important thing in life is to know when to forego an advantage.'

Remain balanced when the other side becomes unbalanced in the heat of negotiation. Let your sober recital moderate the mood. Untangle the logic of your adversary's position. Isolate his realistic choices and their limits. In other words, make the other side see itself without illusions. You will have started by representing only your own case, but in the process you may become a spokesman for the deal. According to Henry Kissinger, Metternich 'made concessions appear, not as surrenders, but as sacrifices to a common cause'.

When negotiations end, both parties should be happy. But this is rare. They end a little sadder but more sober, wistfully aware of the limits of unreasonable greed. Sadness and wistfulness soon pass, and acceptance supervenes. It is a good round of negotiation when both parties leave the table having given some and taken enough. As after a good meal, it is best to leave replete, but not sated.

Negotiations are not, of course, an exercise in compromise, though many compromises are involved. Negotiations are for a new and hard reality. That is all that remains when gives and takes are long forgotten.

Notes

1 S. Chapman, *The Rise of Merchant Banking*, Allen & Unwin, London, 1984, p. 147.
2 Lorin F. Deland, *Imagination in Business* (1909) in A. E. Saunders and H. Les. Creek (eds), *The Literature of Business*; Harper and Brothers, New York and London, 1937.
3 Emily Dickinson, *The Complete Poems*, ed. Thos H. Johnson, Faber & Faber, London, 1975.

4

Business and the Attributes of Taxation

The Ways of Taxation

The twelfth-century scholar, John of Salisbury, thought that tax gatherers were the bowels of the body politic, and, like bowels, ought not to remain unevacuated for long. Apart from a sole right to force, the government's right to tax has, throughout history, been the most jealously guarded monopoly of all. In this, no government – republican, royal, socialist or capitalist – has differed from its neighbour.

It is not so much that we hate paying taxes. In moderation, they are good for us as a form of compulsory altruism. Not only do we have the satisfaction of paying for the virtues of the state, but there is also a major tutelary benefit in tax legislation. If it were not for tax legislation, we would know less about the financial aspects of our own business. We would know less of what is officially considered respectable. Tax laws are written and cleverly revised to prevent escape from tax liability. They are designed to keep both cat and mouse alive – the cat perhaps more alive than the mouse – but still, alive. Whether the price of such lessons is excessive is another matter. At any rate, we may take some comfort from the fact that taxes are what we have to pay for the privilege of being allowed to make a profit.

Far too much time is spent by businessmen in trying to reduce the tax bill by manipulation and manoeuvre. Generally, if the amount of tax saved is close to the amount spent in saving it, abandon the attempt. Even when the amount saved is greater than the amount spent saving it, the attempt may turn out to be expensive when the cost of time and effort is included in the reckoning – time that might have been devoted to one's profits. The return per hour is usually higher.

We began, after all, as experts in our own field of business, not as experts on taxation. And when we started relatively poor – with work and hope and luck – did we not then say that we would be content one day to pay the taxes of a millionaire? The resolution did not survive, but it does no harm to be reminded of it.

There is no need for excessive scruple. If, *without relinquishment of chosen policy*, one can add the additional advantage of lower taxes, so much the better. Unfortunately, instead of looking straight ahead, looking at taxes means looking over one's shoulder, and that, generally, is not the right direction.

Taxes are more than just money which the government takes for its own purposes. They are also an expression of social policy, and their pattern reflects social purposes. The purposes, we grant, are mostly amiable.

Tax policies may sometimes have social consequences exactly as intended. But they may also be far from those intended. One such unintended consequence arises from the very proliferation of tax laws: when making a tax return, it has become virtually impossible for a great number of people with many-sourced incomes to do without the services of tax experts, whose number is now legion.

Our tax systems were often born of muddled history and were nurtured on muddled thought. Without muddle, company taxation would not exist. Official reasoning is that corporations are persons (even though only legal persons) and should be taxed as such. Never mind that no corporation has ever fallen in love. Person it is, therefore consumer it is, and shall pay tax.

It is not logically possible to tax a consumer called a company or corporation, because companies, by definition, are producers, not consumers. Governments can, of course, deliberately use companies as tax farmers or tax gatherers – and this they do. The knowledge that in the long term and on the wider scale of the national economy, companies pass the burden on to customers in one way or another, is swept under the rug of fiscal convenience. Companies are tax gatherers rather than tax payers; and that is all they are. It has been argued that this proposition is not clear-cut in practice. But the existence of the argument only confirms the existence of muddle.

Company tax is a double tax: first the company is taxed on its profits and then any remaining profits are taxed as private income when paid out as dividend. One year, in the case of one small business, this would have meant about 42 per cent effective tax on company profits, followed by a 56.36 per cent effective tax on the remainder as personal income tax, and would have left the sole proprietor with an amount of $25.31 on each $100 of profits before tax. This remainder would then have had to be reduced by local taxes. All this tax burden was incident in the United States of America, a country said to demand less tax than many others.

Then, from necessity, came the advice of the proprietor's chartered accountant. A selection of legally approved exemptions were considered and adopted. From the alchemy of the Emerald Tablets of the tax laws he extracted some gold to save. But why, one asks, why first have many suspect laws that impose needlessly heavy burdens, and then more suspect laws for making them less heavy?

This chartered accountant, a man of honour, lived in deserved comfort on the work he did for this corporation and many corporations like it. He was joined by the company's attorney, friend and mentor, who also wanted for little, and also deserved all that he had. Millions like us cannot do without thousands like them. Is this diversion of talent of a nation's ablest people – accountants, tax attorneys, actuaries – really the intent of parliaments and congresses? Or is it muddled thinking?

Tax and Motives

Taxation in the United States, and by and large in other Western states, has these effects:

It shortens our perspectives. The government wants its money annually. In turn, outside shareholders and recipients of annual bonuses demand it, too. We must therefore account for our corporate income every twelve months. But where is the perennial perspective which comes in neat and convenient annual portions?

The manner in which taxes are levied makes for myopic plans: for trimming rather than for building; for short-run and windfall returns; for quick fixes rather than for steady development, for chapters rather than for books.

It would make little difference in tax yield if corporate tax returns were made every, say, three years for the preceding three. Tax would be payable in twelve quarterly instalments instead of four as now. It would make for a longer-term view by businesses, and would reduce the government's tax-gathering apparatus. Fewer revenue agents and computers would suffice, and the cost of collection would reduce. Fewer accountants and tax experts would be needed by business, even though continuous internal accountancy and annual dividends would continue. In a world which is short of highly qualified people, talented men would be released from the surveillance of wealth to its creation.

It modifies our values. When a profit is made by a trading company with few physical assets, what do we do to avoid paying our beloved government too much in tax? We buy expensive cars and refurbish our offices splendidly so as to make use of depreciation and investment allowances. We entertain more, or claim we do. We think of establishing offices in exotic tax havens until we find that the attractions are not worth the effort. In other words, we waste our company's money. It goes against the grain of normal reasoning, but such is the topsy-turvy world of taxes.

It reduces accumulation. A privately or closely held corporation in the USA which has accumulated a worthwhile amount of money is not permitted to continue to accumulate more. Instead of allowing retained earnings to be saved – in a country with a notoriously low savings rate – the money must, beyond a point, be made available for taxation – by disbursement as dividend or by way of higher salaries. We are not permitted to save enough to equip, say, a manufacturing company, or to make another worthwhile productive investment. Is this, one asks, to teach us some particular virtue? And if so, which one?

Taxation, for good or ill, makes tax legislation become similar everywhere. If one country tax lightly, and the other tax its citizens doubly, the first can have no advantage from its lower taxes and will increase them to equal the second's. And so the heavier hand in one descends on all. Would that it worked as well the other way; beginning with the tax revolt called Proposition Thirteen in California in the late seventies, the lighter hand has started its necessary and welcome mild ascent.

Meanwhile, it is not in the least surprising that there are those in this world who have decided that the best play in the global tax casino is to live in one country, keep their capital in another and let their income from it accumulate in a third.

When taxation becomes an unintended ballot, as it became in the later Roman Empire (disadvantageously to the tax payer in a declining economy), and in the Moorish Spain of the Middle Ages (advantageously to the tax payer in a flourishing economy); or as it also (disadvantageously to the tax payer) became in postwar Britain, many of whose artists and writers lived abroad because of unconscionable taxes; or as in Germany, many of whose companies would prefer to be based in Switzerland or Luxemburg; when all this is so, then the philosophy of taxation – this poorest of philosophies – bears re-evaluation.

Consider in rough outline the warning example of the Roman Empire. Emperor Diocletian chose to reform the tax system in the early fourth century. The value of the denarius had steadily depreciated amid considerable inflation. Neither then nor later did Rome learn how to cure inflation. It was, therefore, impossible for Diocletian to base taxes on rates expressed in terms of money. And so Diocletian decided to base taxes physically on the *iugum*, an area of land that a team of draft oxen pulling a plough could work in one day. It happened that two head of oxen ploughing (a *iugum*), needed the head (or *caput*), of a ploughman to direct them. Since the *iugum* was a taxable unit, and since a *iugum* was useless without a *caput*, the *caput* had to be included in the unit. The reason for the inclusion was compelling: when taxes grew unbearable, *caputs* had a habit of escaping. And when a *caput* departed, his purse was sure to do the same. Hence, to maintain a taxable conjugation of *iugum*, or yoke, with *caput*, or head, it was decreed that no one was to move residence. The burden of the yoke became common to both the land and its tenants.

It is not here maintained that Rome was a parallel to the way things are done today. And yet, even today, when one examines the many tax laws that govern nationality, 'residence permanent', 'residence non-continuous', 'intention to reside', 'abode', 'domicile of choice', 'domicile of origin', 'domicile of incorporation', 'business transacted in', et cetera, it becomes evident that so far as taxes are concerned, the *iugum* and the *caput* are not permitted to be very far apart.

In many cases government today may not itself have intended the social and administrative consequences of a specific act of taxation. Parliamentarians passing laws are not always aware of the nature of the bureaucracies into whose hands they put the execution of their laws: in the case of taxes too often into the hands of zealots. The zealotry is no better for being practised by personally honest men. (We can remind ourselves that none was more persecutorial than the honest Puritans.) Bureaucrats are professional patriots. Their loyalty belongs to their immediate paymaster, the state, and no longer directly to the people. In the hands of civil services the well-intentioned laws of parliaments frequently undergo a phenomenon known to metal workers: work-hardening.

Parliaments and congresses intended that tax be paid by honest declaration, and that failure to declare, and dishonest declaration – and only these – should be severely punished. But collectors of taxes, suspecting that one man may benefit unfairly against others, can always find some equitable principle to justify a prior inquisition. For example, a friend, an honest German businessman, was asked what he had done with the tax-paid money in his account in 1983. 'What business,' said he, 'is it of yours to question me on *my* money – money on which my tax was paid and which is now at my free disposal? I shall in due course declare what income I derive from it – if, that is, I do not choose to spend it on frivolous living.' The reply he had from the collectors of taxes for the Federal Republic of Germany was that they wanted to know what he intended to do with the money *in case* he might feel tempted to withhold an honest declaration at a later date.

No doubt the collectors would plead that they were only trying to be fair, since it would not do to have some men cheat at the expense of other tax payers. This is the kind of even-handedness which makes for heavy-handedness. Germany is genuinely democratic now. But her civil service has yet to become accustomed to the fact that she is no longer a Prussian state; that The State is no longer to be considered morally superior to its citizens; that the civil service and the police are not the supreme dispensers of nursery justice; and that the opinions of their Hegel, their Fichte and their Treitschke must no longer prevail. One does not blame the Federal Republic alone: the tendency of administrators to practise prior restraint is to be found in France and in the USA and Britain.

But a democracy cannot fare well if the enforcement of its humane and reasonable laws is not equally humane and reasonable. Since tax laws cannot define all individual situations, gaps remain which are open to the interpretation of the administering agency. Such, for example, is the case in the USA, where the Internal Revenue Service is entitled to make a ruling, asked or unasked. The determination may be made by a 'private letter ruling', and although these letters are published and are available as precedent, they cannot be so used. The IRS may change its ruling in similar or analogous cases, and may plead a different principle if it so wishes. And in these ways, we are led into administrative justice, a justice of the gaps.

We are also led into a proliferation of experts, of tax advisers, of chartered accountants, of international and domestic tax lawyers, on whom we must call to read the tea leaves of official opinion before the tea is poured. Administering agencies tend to go to the limits of their powers, and we arrive at tolerant democracies intolerantly run.

There is an arrogance of power: 'If we do not hear from you or receive the return(s) with full payment within ten (10) days from the date of this letter,' writes the Department of Taxation of the Commonwealth of Virginia (Thomas Jefferson's state) in pursuit of a small amount of tax, 'we will take one or more of the following actions to collect the liability: Summon you to appear with your records; proceed in court under a *criminal warrant*; recommend *revocation* of your certificate of registration *to conduct business in this State*; issue an assessment based on such information as may be available; or *any other action authorized under the law*. We hope none of these actions will become necessary.' (May 1987. Author's emphases. Verbatim and complete.) It is unnecessary to suppose that Thomas Jefferson would have approved of this display of overwhelming force in the precautionary defence of one of the minor purses of American Democracy.

There is no trust:

after thirty years, no simple, unsupported statement of mine is admissible in connection with matters of taxation. I must fill in every form; I must give every detail; I must recapitulate every item. No such thing as a character is known in public affairs. I may be marked up in the highest grade in every inquiry office in the world; I may be classified by the merchants as worthy of any credit; I may win the highest position among my fellows; but I can never get a good mark of any kind from this thing called the State.[1]

There is at times a little madness in them:

When, some years ago, the author sold his house in the USA and instructed the attorney-of-escrow to send the proceeds to him abroad, a requirement arrived from an official revenue agency telling him to certify that he was 'not a non-resident'.

Certifying that one is not a non-resident would seem not to be dissimilar from saying that one is a resident. This he was, and was prepared to confirm it. But that is not what he was asked to certify. He was asked to affirm a double negative: 'I am not a non-resident.'

Using the same reasoning, he now affirms that he is also prepared to certify that he is not non-existent; in other words, that he exists. If pressed, he is prepared to swear to both propositions, provided he is still existent, that is to say, not non-existent, at time of certification. In the event of his ceasing to exist prior to certification (for whatsoever reason including death) the government may accept the statement he now makes that he shall then not be a resident, or not 'not a non-resident'.

Note

1 Ernest J. P. Benn, *Confessions of a Capitalist*, Hutchinson, London, 1925, p. 271.

Section 2

Politics and Business

Preamble

After matters mostly internal to business in the last section, this section turns to the often uneasy relationship of business with its landlords: states and governments.

What states and governments guard is some established order or other. But the values behind the particular orders are various: the Dictatorship of the Proletariat; the Purity of the Race; God's Dominion on Earth; the Divine Right of Kings; the One True Faith; Liberty and Democracy; Liberty, Equality and Fraternity; Life, Liberty, and the Pursuit of Happiness; the Sanctity of Property; Law and Order; the preservation of Union, Republic, Kingdom, Commonwealth, Empire (as may be the case) from Mob Rule, from the Rule of Tyrants, from the Arrogant Rich, from the Arrogant Aristocracy, from the Oppressing Bourgeoisie. It has been the fate of business to live through them all and to have survived.

Some values defended by authority have been strange: the Younger Pliny, in the first century AD, complained that nothing is more unfair than equality. An English nobleman, fewer than two centuries ago, was coarsely prepared to 'let wealth and commerce, laws and learning die, but give us back our old nobility.' Aristotle justified mastery over the one who is 'by nature a slave'; for St Augustine slavery was the logical result of Man's Fall; for St Thomas slavery was man's deserved chastisement. Every value has had its distinguished defenders.

Governments frequently set a bad example of civility: they often act like philistines to please those voters who are. Their standards of housekeeping are sometimes suspect: inflation as a technique to reduce the national debt is publicly condemned, but practised. And so the businessman has always had his reservations about government. Though he could not afford to alienate kings and princes, and though he bowed his head to them, yet his general poise was to doubt and not to yield uncritically to official exhortation. And even today, when most Western governments are democratic, the businessman is still in doubt.

He is not wrong to be doubtful; honest scepticism carries more moral conviction than unquestioning obedience. When he is in doubt, he doubts on; he doubts continuously, vigilantly, kindly, firmly, constructively and practically. He compromises readily when under pressure to be swayed, but even compromise is an expression of his doubt. He doubts political, racial, business, economic and other theories. He knows that cynicism is destructive, but that there is little wrong with scepticism. Even if he thinks that the vessel of government is seaworthy, he reads the manifest of its cargoes carefully, and questions its destinations.

Few saints ever knew more about temptation and the weakness of human nature than does the businessman. And while he is sceptical of authority, he is equally sceptical about himself. Belief in the perfectibility of man is more assumption than he is prepared to make: with a little twentieth-century pessimism, he does not believe that men are destined for perfection. 'Out of the crooked timber of humanity,' Kant remarked, 'no straight thing was ever made.' But there is consolation for him in the belief that strength need not come from perfection. The crooked timber of which he, too, is made, is usually strong enough.

He believes in freedom and individualism. Individualism, Keynes tells us, if it can be purged of its defects and abuses, is the best safeguard of personal liberty in the sense that, compared with any other system, it greatly widens the field for the exercise of personal choice. It is also the best safeguard for the variety of life, the loss of which is the greatest of all losses of the totalitarian state. This variety, he says, preserves the traditions which embody the most secure and successful choices of former generations; it colours the present with the diversification of its fancy; and, being the handmaid of experiment as well as of tradition and of fancy, is the most powerful instrument to better the future.[1]

He does not, however, delude himself that these 'most secure and successful choices of former generations' made good beginnings. He is aware that much of what is now normal in our market system came from forbidden and cruel events. He is not blind to the fact that our bright and shining phoenixes rose from the ashes of some ugly birds of prey. There was exploitation of women and children; the enclosures of common lands that send thousands from villages to dismal poverty. There were depressions, repressions, revolutions, pollutions, ghettos, sweatshops. History may not teach him much, but it does teach him that some events he may have thought impossible, inconceivable, improbable and unlikely were possible, conceivable, probable and likely.

Which also means that much that is still impossible, inconceivable, improbable and unlikely has been reserved by history for probable occurrence. In hindsight, history may not be a game of chance, but the businessman knows that it is imperfectly predictable in prospect. He also knows that it is not possible to make progress if one starts from perfection, but, seeing that this never happens and that he has always to start from very imperfect situations, progress *is* possible, and he will see to it that it happens.

He knows, also, that an excess of any one virtue is itself no virtue. Thrift, for example, if taken to extremes, deprives others of income. The excessive contemplation of beauty leads to the neglect of people. An excess of action destroys caution. An excess of caution destroys action. An excess of piety often ends in resignation; this, too, destroys action. By itself, sincerity is the least of the virtues. Justice, if taken to extremes, destroys liberty. Liberty, if taken to extremes, destroys justice. According to Lord Acton, a passion for equality makes vain the hope for freedom. And, in a letter he wrote in the late sixteenth century, Dr Thomas Wilson considered any state unfortunate in which nothing was permitted to anybody, but a state in which everything was permitted to everybody was, he thought, even more unfortunate.

He loves liberty, but knows that 'freedom for the wolves has often meant death for the sheep,'[2] and that liberty is, therefore, strictly rationed by all governments – undemocratic as well as democratic. He accepts this – as long as there is room left for a little creative disobedience; it was, after all, Prometheus' disobedience to the gods that brought the gift of fire to mankind. And it was the eleventh-century and later Venetian disobedience of the Church's prohibition against usury that made world commerce and banking possible.

But he asks: Who has more liberty? One who is given free rein by a dictator? Or one who is on a tight rein in a democracy? Is there a difference between *how much* one is governed and *by whom* one is governed? He is concerned by the unceasing growth of regulation within democracy. He has reached the point at which the first question – how much we are governed – becomes pressing for him. There are too many levels of government, too many bureaucrats, too many regulations, too much taxation. Some countries now take in taxes more than 50 per cent of the gross domestic product of their nation. He continues to struggle for a cure but suspects that perhaps there is none, and that finding fault with one judge does not necessarily ensure justice by another. So, while protesting, he puts up with it.

Still, he instinctively prefers democracy, because no amount of benevolence in a dictator can guard against his wilfulness. He distrusts any monolithic state that justifies its own legitimacy by some unalterable social theory – whether it is rule by the Divine Right of Kings or by Marxism-Leninism. His common sense quietly tells him that no rod, however thick, can hold a glass-hard castle of this kind, however strong, up in the air forever. His argument is that it is better to let a hundred flowers bloom than to try to grow one that is perfect. Because, if there is only one flower, one cannot tell that it is perfect.

Notes

1 J. M. Keynes, *The General Theory of Employment Interest and Money*, Macmillan, London, 1936, p. 380.
2 Quoted by Isaiah Berlin in *Four Essays on Liberty*, Oxford University Press, Oxford, 1969, p. xlv.

5

Politics around Business

Politics and Business

Once, when a discussion turned to the subject of Heaven and Hell, the author Jean Cocteau excused himself from offering an opinion on the grounds that he had friends in both places. The businessman, too, suspects that, of his business friends, more are politically in one of these regions than in the other. He is, therefore, reluctant to discuss politics in business company.

Businessmen rarely do; they feel that it may harm the silent professional consensus which exists between them. And so they are careful and talk instead about the market. There are, one can be sure, many business friends of ten or more years standing, who know all there is to know about each other – except each other's politics. Now that active involvement in business is behind or beyond this former businessman, he will not have to pay much of a price for voicing an opinion: his ultimate consignment to one or the other of Cocteau's regions will be adjudged on different grounds.

Still, we can suppose that there is a temptation for businessmen to absorb this or that current political philosophy. Not merely can we suppose it, we know it, and businessmen are certainly not exempt from it. But there is a cautionary label on the political bottle which tells us that the contents may be dangerous to our health and our wealth, and that indiscriminate use may cause partial blindness to reality.

Businessmen cannot help becoming worldly philosophers. They are world-immersed. They sense the moods of time and commerce. A point of view develops. What other occupations are better suited to such reflection? Not that of theologians; their reference is to Heaven, quite another world. Not that of philosophers; they rearrange the meaning of truth from time to time to give eternity a dusting. Not that of politicians, who have to choose between the things they would themselves elect and the public which elects them. Not that of gossip columnists and social diarists; they concern themselves with a floating world.

As observers of mankind whose living depends on their accuracy of judgement, there is no other occupation as closely involved with conduct as that of businessmen. But unlike theologians, philosophers, politicians and columnists, businessmen cannot afford to be excessively judicial. The market buys; it is the only well of profit. The market does not wish to be judged – it wishes to be used. That may not be justice; it just is.

There are, as said, in most businessmen's lives imps of temptation pulling to the Left and to the Right. Their brief conclusion is ambivalent; they dare not be unyielding and intolerant – by conscience; equally, they dare not refuse the discipline of sober-mindedness. They – or many of them – are, therefore, not disciples of that school of benevolent liberalism which believes that Christ's example on how to feed great multitudes on a few loaves and fishes can be repeated. They tend not to believe that the world will be made more perfect by endless pourings from the jug of human kindness. But neither do they believe the opposite.

The world may, indeed, become fairer through institutionalized generosity, but not always better. Marxist societies claim social fairness. But businessmen want to be spared the fairness of shared misery, and they want to be spared brilliant revolutionary social visions which, when applied, make life dull, unchanging, stale.

Nor do all of them want to be disciples of red-necked social philosophies which would have them convinced that even the Ten Commandments can be improved by the omniscient Market; that the Market is both efficient *and* just, and can do no wrong; and that wealth will of itself trickle down from well-filled purses to the deserving (the deserving being often defined, by circular argument, as those who have well-filled purses).

Now it may be said that, being undedicated to either proposition, they are sitting on the fence. They, on the contrary, claim that they are standing where the fence used to be. Business is about the removal of fences and not about being on either side of them. In Emily Dickinson's words, business is a religion that doubts as fervently as it believes.

All this is not to say that businessmen should choose to be politically toothless. It is to say, however, that it seems best to use the same criteria of earthy common sense towards ideology as they daily use for judging business. When presented with some 'perfect' ideology, it is probably best to be as sceptical as the young woman who, on hearing a sermon on the Immaculate Conception, said that she saw little advantage in it. And if in doubt, it is good to read the cautionary label again and stay off the bottle. Someone has to remain sober enough to do the driving.

The Democracy of Money

Dr Samuel Johnson sensibly remarked that there were few ways in which a man can be more innocently employed than in making money. One must be grateful to him; the press is rarely as kind to business as he was. One can agree with critics that a system based on making money is the worst in the world – except for all the others. Money-making is not the best kind of democracy but, being open to all talents, it is a democracy of sorts.

Even though making money is innocent employment for any one person, it does not follow that a society based on commerce only is also good. One must not assume that what is good for one is good for all. What is good for General Motors may not necessarily be good for the United States. Profit is not a bad thing; still, the thought of profit-making saints, judges, generals, priests, policemen, presidents, prime ministers, soldiers, public servants, civil servants, parliamentarians and statesmen is very discomforting. And while one can agree that executives should be able to offer their services and skills freely, one does not agree that executioners should do the same.

No society based on the business system is by itself impeccable. Not every value is for sale; for this one should be truly grateful. Nationhood is not for sale, nor the Rights of Man, nor a clean natural environment. Poverty, sickness and hunger must be dealt with; they are the indignity for some which denies the claim to dignity for others. And despite all good intentions, fortune and the economy have unintended and corrupting consequences which the market system alone cannot put to rights. Good individual decisions do not necessarily add up to a good society. We are always forced to live somewhere between the sanctity of the Ten Commandments and the profanity of auction rooms.

It is sobering to remember that the great depression, which started with the stock-market crash in 1929, took place when business dealings were almost unfettered by laws and regulations. Though some of us were children then, we still remember the misery of those days and we ask, please, for no repetition. Yet in this age of free and enormous global money flows, we are once more faced by the fact that money does not manage itself.

Politics and Capitalism

Capitalism is not any one man's invention. It has no unity, it is unusually diffuse, mostly inelegant, frequently illogical, sometimes disjointed. It has no heroes; no gentlemen like Marx or Lenin; only thousands of players with lesser names like yours or mine, Rothschild or Carnegie.

Capitalism is not a system but a critical procedure. It is a testing ground for what can and what cannot be done with money, knowledge and imagination. It is a continuous critique which has success as its judge and society as its jury.

There is communism and there is democratic capitalism. There are people who will agree that they are communists. There are fewer who would agree that they are capitalists. If I say that I am a member of the Salvation Army, a bridge club, a political party or a society for the preservation of ancient monuments, I am saying that I belong to a company of like-minded people gathered for a common purpose. But when I am called a capitalist, it tells me nothing of any common purpose I may have with other capitalists. I am accused by Marxists of living off the surplus value of my employees. It has not occurred to them to ask whether my employees may not be making a good living off the surplus value of my unremitting labour. I also know that other capitalists live off the surplus value I generate, and I off theirs; and so who is the hunter and who are the hunted? And when a country of the Eastern Bloc buys my supplies and thus my excellent and cheaper surplus values, who in this world can claim a simon-purity?

Business life asks, every day, for self-discovery and self-examination. Democratic capitalism is a self-transforming category. It is likely to remain imperfectly defined because it is transmuting itself constantly.

Despite the cold sweat of entrepreneurial anxiety, this adds a little interest to daily work.

By contrast, Leninism and later national communism is self-defined and, for many years, not visibly self-transforming. It started with a vision and got stuck with Stalin, and since then with a Party Apparatus and probably with a Military-Industrial Complex also. In fairness, its economic performance, in the USSR at least, has improved: each working person's annual income (in 1985) was just a little higher than that of each Irishman's and Puerto Rican's, and just a little less than half a German's. So, one should admit, has the Soviet government's respect for law since Stalin – with some remarkable denials retained.

But the red-blooded vision of the Revolution became an anaemic recitation of increases in quantity of coal produced and public admonitions about the poor quality of socks. One rightly suspects a 'people's democracy' in which ordinary telephone directories were a state secret and in which copying machines were under official lock and key until recently.

All this confirms one in the conviction that none is as conservative as he who conserves a revolution.

Politics and Communism

An indictment of the communist system does not turn on economic performance. After the devastation of the War, the USSR has, after all, become the third-largest economy in the world – far behind the United States and a little behind Japan. In international trade, she is a shrewd buyer, and an honourable payer. We must not mind that she forbids the existence of a merchant-class; that is more her loss than ours.

Until the late eighties, the indictment turned on other things: a canting redefinition of the meaning of ordinary freedoms; pharisaical self-righteousness; the hallowing of man in the mass but disdain for men as individuals; the embalming of last century's truths in the mausoleum of the present one; moralism towards outsiders but dissembling towards her own citizens; dullness; theocracy; inertia; the taking of once not ignoble ideas and not unworthy ideals and turning them into idols of compulsory worship; the celebration of ashes instead of fire; permanent condemnation to a life of moral and economic siege; the claim to a science of socialism, but its maintenance, not by a consensus of science, but by a concert of policemen.

The preceding words were written before the changes made by Gorbachev became manifest. He has made one great change already: irreversibly, communism is no longer a religion. His Russia, the Russia of Lenin, then Stalin, then Khrushchev, then interregnum, now Gorbachev, is running to a Revised Fourth Edition which we shall shortly acknowledge.

Still, on the principle that even fallen angels have their uses, one must ask whether the existence of communist dictatorships has done the world no good at all. Since the Second World War, the existence of the rival induced Western nations to be reasonably good allies, better than they might otherwise have been. Because war between the West and the East had become unthinkable, a second miracle happened; there have been no wars between the nations of the West for over forty years (except for a minor Greek–Turkish skirmish). France and Germany are the best of friends. Britain and Turkey adhere to the same treaty. Twelve European nations are joined in close union. Politically, Japan has become a Western nation. Peace has brought about, first through the Marshall plan and since then in other ways, help between nations. It has encouraged the free flow of funds and investments in the West. If it continues, economic nationalism may some day abate.

Far from preventing it, the East has, by its own obduracy, nurtured the unity of the West. Instead of commercial autarky, high tariffs and protectionism, trade has become more free.

We do not have full free trade yet; only 40 or so per cent of international commerce is 'free'. Nor is what we have of it due to this one circumstance alone. But what might have been the state of economic narrowmindedness without the past adversary whose earlier antagonism had to be resisted? Our response was to foster international interdependence, aid between nations and an attitude of greater liberality. Business must not complain, and the merchants of the world may delight. They had nothing to lose but constraints.

Unlike monolithic systems, the business system is a patchwork quilt. It is far from perfect, but there is hope. It can amend itself, and can accommodate many and various values. Within it, we can express private international charity. Where, by contrast, is private aid from, say, individual Bulgarians for starving Africans?

Our system is participatory in so far as mass societies can be participatory; even between elections, the media are our permanent debate. Private and individual initiatives are neither encouraged nor discouraged, but may contend for public acceptance. In it, there is a continuous evolution of beliefs, ideas, tastes, arts and invention. Given the vigilance of its citizens, fundamental human values are withheld from vulgar inroads.

These are great virtues, and we must be conscious of them. We must not, as businessmen, forget our role in this system and our duty towards its maintenance. Given no wars, the winning system will ultimately be judged, not on economic grounds alone, nor on military strength, but on humanity.

The Soviet Union and the Future of Business

One must take it for granted that Russia at peace with the rest of the prosperous world is a prosperous Russia at peace with herself. Her dilemma has so far been the mismatch between her ideals and her structures. Her early ideal was the dignity of the common man; her later structure was the ruthless enforcement of his obedience. Lenin, writing on liberty in the late summer of 1917, said that under communism men will gradually become accustomed to observing the elementary rules of social intercourse that have been known for centuries – without force, without compulsion, without subordination, without the special coercive apparatus which is called the state. It was not to be, and the people did not become 'accustomed'. Only nine years after Lenin said it, his favourite, Bukharin, later killed by Stalin, now about to be given life again by Gorbachev, complained that the communist party in Russia was 'a completely declassed class . . . a bureaucratic clique entirely detached from the masses', totally lacking ideals.

But it would be wrong to believe that her new democratic thrust means the same to her as to Western nations. The Western cry is for political decency, but above all for liberty. The Russian cry is also for human decency, but above all for social order – with love of Russia in the first rank, but with political liberty a contentious, almost suspect, issue of the second rank. And for this reason if no other, Russia will probably retain her socialism less as an ideology than as a unifying discipline.

As to her other reason, she will retain socialism and what she calls 'democratic centralism' from economic necessity. We shall shortly (chapter 8) see that the theocracy of the Middle Ages was followed by mercantilism. Now that Russia is shedding her dishonoured dogmas, mercantilism may also be her destiny in the years ahead.

The Soviet Union is not one but two economies. The first economy supplies elaborate plant and ingenious arms to the Third World. To this world, the USSR is a highly advanced economy. The second economy is, however, unable to supply, in either quantity or quality, enough for her own people. Nor does it produce more than a trickle of acceptable goods which the Western world might want to buy from her.

Her annual exports, including the Eastern Bloc, are 300 dollars per head of her population – perhaps a little more. Her annual exports to the West, also *per caput*, are only about 100 dollars. If one excludes oil, gas and other fuels, it is only about a quarter of this hundred. Compare this with West Germany's total exports of over 3,000 dollars per head of population; Britain's, France's and Japan's (each) of nearly 2,000 and the USA's of nearly 1,000. And if one takes the Soviet Union's total goods trade – *per caput* exports *and* imports – it is about one ninth West Germany's, one sixth France's or Britain's, one quarter the USA's or Japan's, but about nine times China's.[1]

When, therefore, one of the mightiest countries of the world is now determined to become an equal power in the world's trade and industry, but is so far behind, its choice for decades is bound to be a modified mercantilism: strict control of foreign borrowing but intensive domestically financed investment, control of exchange and foreign trade, the conversion of military to civilian and export production.[2] The influence of Western business in this development will be qualitatively of great importance, but quantitatively limited: the Soviet market is immense, but it cannot pay and may not want to borrow: 'We accepted *détente* with radiant hopes', says Gorbachev, '[w]e even discontinued some of our research and technological developments, hoping for the international division of labor, and thinking that some machines would be more advantageous to buy than to manufacture at home. We were seriously punished for our *naivité*. We decided to put an end to the "import scourge." We started the necessary research and development and the production of what we once proposed to purchase, so Western firms will ultimately be the losers.'[3] This is the voice of mercantilism. There will be 'Socialism in One Country' for some time yet.

There are two visions of her future: the first is Andrew Sakharov's and Mikhail Gorbachev's. The other, different, is Alexander Solzhenitsyn's – and Mikhail Gorbachev's. Sakharov – scientist, humanist, rationalist, progressivist, pluralist, gradualist, guardedly Westernizer, guardedly convergionist, believer in one social-democratic world – speaks for democracy, liberty and planned reform, as does Gorbachev. Solzhenitsyn – writer, Slavophile, moralist, traditionalist – is a critic of Western materialism, consumptionism and 'rationalistic humanism' (i.e. Western capitalism). Justice, truth, 'organic' wholeness, 'the healing of the [Russian] soul', and every man's devotion to social duty, matter more to him than the deified truths of Marxism, democracy, industrialization and political liberty. His vision, as in part Gorbachev's also, is of a decent and paternalistic country with a law-abiding and honest government, which shepherds a people that will no longer applaud a lie, and will not lie itself.

The vastness of their land inspires the writings of Andrew Sakharov and Alexander Solzhenitsyn, both. Despite their differences, both are anti-communist. Both embrace a characteristically Russian belief in the leadership of a benevolent intelligentsia, and so does Gorbachev. Both are men of iron will, and so is Gorbachev.

The interest Western business has in these developments is a world at peace and commerce free of barriers. There will be more profit in such a world than in direct trade with the Soviet Union.

Gorbachev's mind, more than any Western statesman's, is a business mind. It seeks sober results bereft of illusion. It is prepared to write off losses. It is determined to make the future profitable. His new vision has the goodwill of all Western nations. The future must decide whether it has the will and goodwill of the Soviet Union's own people. But let us not forget that of the Great Powers of the nineteenth century – Austria, Prussia, France, Britain, Russia – only Russia has remained great.

There is a third and very disconcerting reason why Soviet Russia may choose to keep her socialism. It is a reason still hidden from herself, perhaps. As has been shown in two world wars, and will be shown again if insufficiency in times of peace becomes the general estate of earth, capitalism does not cope well with scarcity unless it turns itself into a command economy. This, Soviet Russia has been for many years; she knows the politics of insufficiency quite well, and, perhaps not quite as well, its economics.

Notes

1 Based on the United Nations *International Statistics Yearbook*, figures for 1984; and Michael Ellman, *The USSR in the 1990s*, Economist Intelligence Unit Special Report No. 1152, London, February 1989. Figures for 1986 and 1987.
2 In addition, other internal changes: a new emphasis on services, better transport and other infrastructures, an emphasis on quality and reliability, a reduction of the huge budget deficit, a controlled transition to domestic market prices, *uskorenie* (acceleration) where it does not conflict with *perestroika* (reconstruction) and, above all, more food, goods and comfort.

    If these steps succeed, if also a massive invasion of foreign joint ventures injects capital for export industries, and if the Soviet Union reduces waste by half in her 150-million-tonne steel industry to the point at which she has many million tonnes available for foreign sale, she could double her exports. (She would, however, ruin the steel industries of many countries by so doing.)
3 Mikhail Gorbachev, *Perestroika*, Collins, London, 1987.

6

Politics in Business

Politics and Generosity

Businessmen try to be mostly realists. By a realist one means someone who is canny enough to believe that a little careful unselfishness – in the right places and at the right time – is not a form of idealism, but a form of necessary realism. With a little care, it can even make a profit. Despite the charges of egotism and moral coarseness which are frequently raised against businessmen, we find many to be generous givers – those, at least, who have gone through the mills of life.

Nature has laws but none concerning justice. She has left justice and humanity for us to add. And while business is not there for humaneness, it can hardly function well without it. Not many, however, believe that corporations and companies should try to be miniature welfare societies. Loyalty to their staff, decent incomes, recognition, contributions to retirement, health insurance for employees and managers: these, where they can, they should provide. But no meticulous paternalism is asked of them.

In the hands of myopic managers, corporate welfare can be a means of bonding employees to the corporation at lower than average wages. In the longer view, this is a policy of little value to either employer or employee. It is frequently the mark of corporate senility. At labour negotiations, company negotiators are readier to grant welfare payments and other non-cash concessions, because they represent money later, not money now. And so the ratchet-wheel of future overheads is cranked and it is left to a future president of the corporation to throw out the catch of the ratchet. This is a difficult manoeuvre and usually means that said president will have to move the operation to Taiwan or Timbuktu or close it down entirely. The best contribution a company can make, for itself and for society, is to make itself efficient, respect its staff and not waste their past work.

Politics and Conservation

It is difficult to understand why some businessmen think of conservation as a virtue, when it is clearly a necessity. One reason offered for being a progressive, G. K. Chesterton once said, is the belief that things naturally tend to grow better. It is not so. The only reason for being a progressive is that things naturally tend to grow worse. All conservatism, he said, is based upon the idea that if you leave things alone you leave them as they are. But you do not. If you leave a thing alone you leave it to a torrent of change. 'If you leave a white post alone it will soon be a black post. If you particularly want it to be white you must be always painting it again; that is, you must be always having a revolution. Briefly, if you want the old white post you must have a new white post.'[1]

There is one kind of man who, in fact, practises the opposite of the conservatism he professes. He is inventive, energetic, unfettered by conventional opinion and innovative. Whatever he may publicly profess, he is in fact a radical in business. His conservatism simply says: 'Government, I am engaged in a dramatic enterprise. Kindly refrain from shifting the scenery while I rehearse the second act.' He is a radical in an old sense of the word: he goes to the root of things. Businessmen must be a yeast and leaven, and enough of it to make the national loaf a bread and not a pancake.

Another kind of man has inhaled the stale night-breath of received ideas. He exhales it, both in his social opinions and in his attitude to work. He is all respectability, a respectability loaded with the usual purple-coloured baggage of prejudice. Of such a self-appointed company retainer there is nothing to say except that he is dangerous. He will clutch at new loyalties as readily as he did at old loyalties. He is the ultimately faithless man.

It is a matter of concern that the internal ambiance in so many older corporations in the United States, and particularly in the countries of the European Community, encourages conformity. Exposed to this, young entrants to management assume that conformity is what being in business is about. It will take them years to see that senior management is not about preserving, but about breaking images. The traditional attitude in British business is that 'father knows best'; in France, that *le patron* knows best; in Germany, that *der Alte* knows best; and that even if, patently, none of these old gentlemen knows best, stupidity is their princely prerogative.

But we must beware: if it does nothing more than pursue its proper aims, business is already the most pervasive social institution in our society. We work in it; we buy from it; the information media are almost wholly maintained from the revenues of its advertising; our cities and towns are largely shaped by it. Its collective influence frames the realities of daily life. Business must shun more influence than this; it needs no more. Its business, as Milton Friedman thought, is to get on with it.

To be 'conservative' in politics and to wish to preserve good institutions is unexceptionable, but to wish to preserve established ways simply because they are established is folly: 'A state without the means of some change is without the means of its conservation,' said the conservative Edmund Burke.

Tradition justifies itself by upholding the good, and not necessarily the old. Not reform, but conservation, is tradition's wariest critic. One remembers one writer's reply to someone who thought that what is, is right: 'except for the absurd consequence that by the same argument all that was, was right'.

Politics and Reform

We must assume, as does the hardy American conservative George F. Will, that there are 'ennobling functions' for government to foster. He may or he may not agree with Dr Samuel Johnson that 'a decent provision for the poor is a true test of civilization', and that poverty certainly destroys liberty, and makes some virtues impracticable and others extremely difficult.

Social improvement has not been, as is commonly supposed, a preoccupation of socialists. Prince Bismarck installed social security in Germany between 1883 and 1889; by 1957, Konrad Adenauer had completed the task. The basic outlines of Britain's present system were devised in 1942, in the midst of the Second World War, in Churchill's government. A precursor of that system was the Conservative Benjamin Disraeli, whose social legislation dates back to 1875, and, in 1911, the Liberal Lloyd George, then Chancellor of the Exchequer. De Gaulle did not install social security in France, but neither did he disturb it, and he was an advocate of industrial democracy. None was a socialist.

It is in the interest of business, as of politics, to have social stability. But for the fact that provisions for the unemployed were in place in the early eighties, it is possible that neither Mrs Margaret Thatcher in Britain nor Herr Helmut Kohl in Germany, both conservatives, would have had a chance of re-election. And one would guess that President Ronald Reagan, when re-elected in 1984, succeeded because no hordes of destitutes were roaming the streets in revolt against the rest of the American nation. It is an irony of welfare democracy that it gives political continuity and conservation a chance; without it, who knows who or what would rule. Except that it would not be moderation.

A nation which will not take elementary care of its unfortunates is hardly likely to remain for long a nation loved by its citizens. It would at best be a collection of accidental presences. On the other hand, as Keynes said, 'the important thing for Government is not to do things which individuals are doing already, and to do them a little better or a little worse; but to do those things which at present are not done at all.'

Every political and economic system has its contradictions and dilemmas. The dilemma of democracy is that, being relatively free, citizens' uses may become abuses. It is the most ancient of dilemmas. But it has not deterred us from unleashing the talents of our citizens. On balance, democracy, using the business system to unfold the productive talents of its people, has proved the most agreeable society to live and work in. Energy and talent, and the right to their display, are worthy assets of mankind.

Some years ago, an eminent journalist asked the very effective Prime Minister of Singapore, Lee Kwan Yew, why, having once been a socialist, he did not nationalize his industries. Mr Lee answered drily that he could scarcely find enough talent to run his government, never mind his industries.

Liberty, Privacy and Property

Is the right to privacy a part of liberty? Privacy, after all, 'as something sacred in its own right, derives from a conception of freedom which . . . is scarcely older than the Renaissance or the Reformation'.[2] We nevertheless accept privacy as a self-evident part of the Western tradition of liberty.

Emigrants from the USSR to the United States have been known to complain that life in the USA – and life in other Western countries – is a life in isolation. They miss the cosy ease with which they used to find company. What they say in essence is that there are too many doors in the West.

To an extent, privacy is indeed a matter of counting doors, and in turn, having many doors implies having a house and property. Privacy is partly a function, and partly a consequence, of private property.

If privacy is a part of liberty and if privacy is in some way linked to property, then the idea of liberty is also in some way linked to the idea of property. Privacy cannot exist without property; savages constantly live in each others' company, whereas being able to close one's doors on the world outside presumes that one has doors to close.

However, property as a means to privacy and property as a means to power are two different things. The Fathers of the Church, in particular the sixth-century Pope Gregory 'the Great' (known chiefly for the remark that the Angles were not so much Angles as angels – an opinion with which some observers have since been unable to concur), held that property was ours only in trust.

There must, of course, be limits, and the limits to the moral rights of property are set by the moral limits to the powers of property.

The question whether the right to property is a natural right, or a necessary artifice for civilized life, or whether 'property is theft', is more than we can here discuss.

But what happened in communist countries which believed in the abolition of property? Property has become their overwhelming preoccupation.

The Russian revolution, after several waves of expropriations, some of them achieved by the death of millions of peasants, has had to create a planning apparatus and a bureaucracy, mainly to administer property. Its legal code defines the pre-eminent domain of the state to its property – which is to say, of everything ownable. The distinction between state and property has disappeared. The state itself has become a great estate; all the people in it have become guards and gamekeepers for the overlord.

In Western democracies, property has some power, but it is dispersed. But where all property is vested in the state, and is concentrated, property becomes the source of all other powers, including the sustenance of armies and police. Little remains other than property relationships and their protection. The people become keepers of state property. Knowledge becomes state property: copying machines (operated by policemen); large and small news agencies (TASS and demi-TASSes); text books and encyclopaedias with constantly revised history in them. History itself becomes state property. We have come full circle; in a communist state, far more than in a capitalist state, property determines the state's ideology.

In the days to come, in turning the USSR from a command economy to a market-and-profit economy, property will be the greatest obstacle that *perestroika* will encounter. A sense of personal involvement, of personal risk and reward, and above all a sense of ownership, is usually essential to a market economy, in which a myriad centres of initiative take the place of state-owned monoliths. Mr Gorbachev and his successors may find their greatest crises and their greatest ideological, practical and financial problems in this transfer of property from one great fist to thousands of hands.

But to return to business in the West: in 1932 Adolf Berle and Gardiner Means wrote *The Modern Corporation and Private Property*.[3] It was an examination of property when stock-ownership on the one hand and control of the corporation on the other become divided functions. Early ownership had its set of risks *and* duties. But now, argued Berle and Means, stock-holders no longer manage. They only participate in risk. The fiduciary trust of which Pope Gregory spoke, which is one of the duties of ownership, has passed to management. And so, business property is back where it was fourteen centuries ago: in the hands of management, to hold in trust for others. One might remind oneself of this from time to time.

Notes

1 G. K. Chesterton, *Orthodoxy*, John Lane, The Bodley Head, London & New York, 1909.
2 Isaiah Berlin, *Four Essays on Liberty*, Oxford University Press, Oxford, 1969, p. 129.
3 Berle and Means, *The Modern Corporation and Private Property*, Macmillan, New York, 1932.

PART II

Past

Section 3

Movements that Shaped Business

Preamble

Enterprise refashions the world at least once in every two generations. It thrusts and drives; but it is also driven. Its future, tautened by its past, coiled up inside its present, untwines – urging and propelling it.

But though business is one of the great shapers of the Western world, businessmen were not, nor are they now, its dominators. This section all too briefly tells of a past in which commerce rose in Europe, was dominated by ecclesiastical or political power; was sometimes overwhelmed by it; spread to other continents; was weak at first, then strengthened; discovered that money is not solid but liquid; began in trade, then added industry.

There are several themes. The most perennial theme is the role of trust, reciprocity, consideration and good faith in business. These are now, as they have always been, the implied foundation of commercial dealing. One may, in one's uncertainty, ask whether business with its involutions and complexities, its plots and schemes, its caveats and risks, its triumphs and humiliations, its bluffs and tricks, its brass, hard iron and cold soul, bears any relation to reciprocity and trust. But it does, and it will stand the test of cynical dismissal. Not only was good faith always a very particular stock-in-trade of business, it was also its most practical technique; there could be little trade without it, no exchange without consideration, and no continuity without discharge of obligations.

Colonial America was a case in point. It had a lively trade with Britain, but had little cash and needed credit. Of the metallic coins circulating in the colonies between about the 1650s and the 1750s, few were British pounds, shillings and pence. There were Spanish silver dollars, known as pieces of eight, Seville pieces of eight, Pillar pieces of eight, Peru pieces of eight, doubloons, pistoles, ducatoons, crusadoes, guineas, Johannes and Lyon dollars, and a little wampum, also Massachusetts pine-tree shillings (for thirty-two years, until the British government insisted on its royal prerogative to be the sole minter of coin). There was 'country pay' – grain, beef, pork, tobacco and other barterables. There was also a great deal of ordinary 'trusting'.

In 1690, Massachusetts issued the first paper currency; it was the first not only in America, but also in the British Empire. Other colonies issued more, but there was no unified currency. There were interest-bearing notes, some of which were legal tender, while others were not; there were non-interest-bearing notes, some of which were legal tender for future obligations but not past debts; some were legal tender for all purposes, and others not legal tender between private persons but receivable for public payments. In some instances funds arising from certain sources of taxation were pledged for the redemption of the notes, in others not. In some cases they were payable on demand; in others, at some future time. They were sometimes issued by committees, and sometimes by a specially designated official.[1] Such were the commercial uncertainties of the times.

Yet transatlantic trade, sustained by reciprocal trust, continued. It was in the hands of American merchants who mostly used English merchants as their bankers. These generally allowed twelve months credit without interest added. The length of credit was dictated by the slowness of commercial traffic; the circuit from order, readiness of goods and shipment to sale and settlement was long. Neither colonial nor English merchants had much credit information on the other. One letter written from Bristol in England in 1766, to Newport in Rhode Island, illustrates: 'I must, Dear Sir, make use of your Friendship to favour me in the most Private and Expeditious Manner what your opinion is of Mr Robert Crooke of your place. . . . I have sent Mr Crooke out by way of New York a pretty large Cargo of Goods, without knowing any thing of his Circumstances therefore must trepass [sic] upon your Goodness for your Private Opinion of him which shall be kept by me as an inviolate Secret.'

Earlier, a businessman-scholar of the fifteenth century wrote: 'We kept our promises simply and faithfully and so we became known in Italy and in foreign parts as great merchants.'[2] Earlier still, one Assyrian trader wrote to another about 4,500 years ago: 'If you intend to send your money here to buy goods, and your written order arrives before the money comes, I will buy the wares you designate from my own means and send them to you.'

Business may justly be accused of not having a sense of destiny, a *telos* of its own. But it has, when it chooses, good roads with destinations of its own.

A second theme is the conflict between commerce, and political or ecclesiastical power.

By about 500 BC, for example, Carthage, Corinth, Rhodes, Miletus and Alexandria had ripened to wealth. Many of the polities of Greece were civilizations sustained by commerce. The political empire of the Romans was not inclined to let rich and independent cities challenge it. In the centuries that followed, Roman arms felled or captured them, one by one.

After the fall of Rome, the culture of cities almost vanished in Western Europe. It was not until merchant cities like Luebeck, Venice, Florence, Genoa and Augsburg rose in about the eleventh century, and reached their apogee of wealth and urbanity in about the sixteenth century, that cities again became carriers of culture, learning and accumulation. Then, in the seventeenth and eighteenth centuries, political power reasserted its challenge to commercial power. The second revival of commercial cities was cut short by kings and their armies. This new decline was also gradual. The centralization of the powers of the state came first in Britain and British business was the first to yield. French business yielded next, then, less quickly, Venice and Italian cities. Finally, in the eighteenth century, the Dutch merchant state, until then the greatest commercial empire ever built by man, resigned. Small remnants – Hanse towns like Hamburg, Bremen, Luebeck – held on until they were gelded by Hitler and his absolute state.

For many centuries the advantage of power was tilted entirely to governments and churches, and governments – of the Left and the extreme Left, of the Right and the extreme Right – often made evil use of it. Examples abound: from 1917–1921, Lenin 'bought' foodstuffs from the peasantry and paid in paper. The notes were redeemed in 1924 at one fifty-billionth of their face value.[3] 'Continental' bills were issued by Georgia, Virginia and several other states between 1775 and 1780. Depending on the state, they paid back from 1.25 to 250 dollars on each one thousand dollars borrowed. 'Not worth a Continental' the people still say. Heinrich Wolf of Nuremberg lent all his money in stages to Maximilian I

(1459–1519). Maximilian did not repay any of it and ruined Heinrich. To compensate, turning the knife in the wound, he dubbed Heinrich's son a royal councillor. In the reign of Philip IV 'the Fair' of France (1285–1314), the Knights Templar, lenders to the king, were killed and their riches impounded. Originally 'the Poor Knights of Christ and of the Temple of Solomon', they had – more like Solomon than Christ – become rich bankers and landowners, and were punished for it. In seventeenth- to nineteenth-century Japan, under the Tokugawas, nobles did not have to repay more than one-tenth of their debts to merchants – not unlike ancient Greece about twenty-three centuries earlier, when Solon's *seisachtheia* demanded repayment of a similar portion only (admittedly to save men from passing into serfdom for non-payment of debt).[4]

The conflict between authority and commerce has not ceased in our time; a tendency to control business, and sometimes to usurp it, has not been abandoned even in democracies, let alone the Eastern Bloc. And therefore, whether or not it is the duty of government to keep the people honest, it is certainly the duty of the people to keep the government honest – this being an overwhelming argument in favour of democracy.

The two origins of business – provision of luxury for some, supply of utility for many – is the third theme.

The trade of the Middle Ages was small in relation to the population, and was often limited to medicines and spices for those who could afford them: aloe, agaloch, balsam, camphor, cardamon, purging cassia, costmary, galingale, gallnuts, ginger, laudanum, manna, myrobalan, rhubarb, *succus bituminosus*, saffron, scammony, tragacanth, tutty, zedoary are included in a typical list.[5] True, the origins of capital formation, of credit, the separation of management from ownership, increases in the scale of trade and manufacturing, the growth of professional merchantdom and commercial codes began or revived in the late Middle Ages. The flowering of later centuries would not have occurred without them. Still, most trade was for things desired by the rich. It grew as the mobility of merchants came increasingly to be pitted against the nobility of knights.

Cities rose and crafts moved into the cities. Flanders and Florence, for example, became major textile manufactories with mass production, division of labour, strikes and strike breaking. Between the thirteenth and the fifteenth centuries, the manorial maintenance economy had become a money and exchange economy, and a century later it adopted mercantilism – an alliance of powerful kings with rich deferential men of trade – as doctrine. The royal purple dipped freely into the leather purses of great merchants for its borrowings.

The mercantilist world acquired a taste for luxury. Or, rather, it made the thrilling discovery that luxury was possible. It had not been a virtue in the Middle Ages because thrift had then been the only conceivable reality. The sixteenth century had no need to persuade itself that luxury was a virtue. To persuade itself that thrift was an evil was sufficient. It argued that thrift was a cause of unemployment. Money saved, it reasoned, was money withheld from circulation, therefore thrift was potential income denied to tradesmen and the crafts. This new mode of thought ultimately led to the idea of our modern consumer society and to twentieth-century Keynesian economics.

The productivity of craftsmen in the late Middle Ages and the Renaissance was low. It took centuries to erect and finish a cathedral. Ghiberti worked for forty years on the doors of the baptistery of St John in Florence. Several generations worked to carve the choir stalls. The Sacci family of Milan laboured for over 200 years on the silver for the altar of the cathedral.

With the advent of the Industrial Revolution, craft production for luxury became mass production for utility. In Europe, production had begun with provision for kings, nobles, rich servants of the state and wealthy merchants. This tradition, now partly overgrown, is still faintly in evidence. Mass manufacture of utilitarian objects only came in the eighteenth and nineteenth centuries. But in North America production had been for utility from its beginnings. There, production for luxury came much later. Herein may lie the great difference of outlook between the two continents, and the reason why Europe and Japan have copied America in our century.

Notes

1 See R. A. Foulke, *The Sinews of American Commerce*, Dun & Bradstreet, 1941, Part II.
2 Leon Batista Alberti, *Libro della Famiglia*, (On the Family), 1432.
3 L. E. Hubbard, *Soviet Money and Finance*, Macmillan, London, 1936, p. 3.
4 R. H. Tawney, *Religion and the Rise of Capitalism*, John Murray, London, 1926/1944, p. 60.
5 Wilhelm Heyd, *Geschichte des Levantehandels im Mittelalter*, Stuttgart, 1879, II, pp. 550ff.

7

Freedom and Accountability

Freedom as Trust

This is an age in which we assemble our gods from components, an age in which we grant them presences and offer them dismissals, and an age in which we give them interpretations and reinterpretations. Still, this is not an age of utter cynicism. Western man has 'even survived the shock of discovering than when Utopian dreams are translated into real life the perfect world is still far away'.[1]

Let this be said: there has not been a time in which so many of mankind's energies and talents were used with as much coherence as in our present age. It is not the best of all possible worlds – it is far from that. But it is probably the best of all the actual worlds recorded by history.

There is, in the West, a certain balance now between men's rights and their duties; a certain amount of balance between their rights and the rights of the state; a certain balance in the justice of our laws; a certain amount of civic peace; a certain freedom for business and enterprise. Industry and commerce have achieved some dignity and self-respect. Men in business no longer feel a lowliness of occupation. There is, also, a certain kindliness in mankind now, only about one hundred years old, towards its own aged and ill; and a regard, barely forty years old, for poorer nations. The sum of all compassion – practical, private, national and international – is, if anything, increasing.

The sciences supply knowledge to industries providing goods. The consumer has a voice wherewith to judge the products and services on offer to him. And if the man in the street is not always able to judge well and wisely, there is growing public protection for him against dangerous drugs, adulterated foods, polluted water and polluted air.

We are better informed and better entertained. The arts and music for all tastes can draw on more extensive historical awareness than ever before. The professions are more competent and more earnest. Life is longer, health is better, medicine more efficacious. There is an abundance of books. There is more teaching than in any century that has gone before, more sports and games and recreations. There is more expert assistance for the amateur and the professional, more travel and more income. If we have lost our belief in the Inevitability of Progress and the Perfectibility of Man, we have at least gained the necessary vigilance to make some progress possible and to make mankind more peaceable.

And though, clearly, for every one of these statements there are many exceptions, gaps, imbalances and fears, nevertheless the exceptions are slowly reducing, the gaps narrowing, the imbalances less unaddressed, the fears less unallayed. We know at least what is amiss and what it is that needs amendment.

This is not to say that ours is a golden age. We are still haunted by crime, by a lunatic fringe of perverted political and religious passions, by terrorism, and the debt, the hunger and the poverty of millions. Alien gases fill the air. The menace of unutterable war still hovers over us.

But though not yet for all and not yet stable, this age is a little more golden for the common man than any before it. About one hundred years ago – only about one hundred years ago – serfdom and slavery were universally abolished in the Western world.

Ours is a time of which the future historian may say that in it all mankind's gifts and talents began to flow together. Or he may look back on it and say that it was a false dawn whose rising lustre soon darkened into night. Still, it is not yet an age in which we have surrendered to discouragement.

But while this is not an age of total cynicism or discouragement, business has grown large and ubiquitous, complex and inbred, formal and technical. It often forgets that its foundations stand on the fundamental soil of reciprocal trust and exchange.

Business has no grant of freehold on this soil. It has, perhaps, an old-established grant of leasehold, but the leasehold is conditional on proper tenancy.

Trust is the coin of the realm. It is no less the basic coin of business. Despite interpretations and revisions, integrity is not a machine-made product. There are no ethics factories or mills manufacturing morals. No one, certainly, can be fool enough to believe that morality is the sounding brass and tinkling instrument of trade. On the other hand, the voice of commerce would be either very still or very shrill without it.

Honour above Honesty

Commerce has been made superficially precise by measurement, financial ratios and financial statements. Superficially precise, since no financial statement can account for business that *might* have been gained but has not been gained for lack of what the poet Robert Bridges called the 'masterful administration of the unforeseen'. Lost sales and bungled opportunities do not show on any profit-and-loss account. Money is no substitute for what it buys, and even the best accountancy is no substitute for good management and salesmanship.

Even before the sixteenth century, the merchants of Italy and southern Germany knew how to reckon. But calculation with the use of that most indispensable of instruments, the zero, did not become general until the sixteenth century – although the Italian mathematician Fibonacci had published an account of it in 1202, three hundred years earlier. (An attempt to multiply in Roman numeration will demonstrate some early obstacles to accountancy; for example, XLIV × XVIII = DCCXCII.) We know of the expense book of one William (Wild) Darrell, an Englishman, kept from 16 April to 14 July 1589, and extending to 21 printed pages. Even at this late date Darrell still used Roman numerals: 'May 11th, 1589, Supper. A shoulder of mutton – xvi d. [pence]. 2 Rabbettes – x d. For dressinge ye mutton, rabbettes – viii d. Colde bief – viii d. Cheese – ii d.'

Where a merchant kept such accounts, he usually did it himself at a late and private hour; the secret of his dealings was not to be entrusted to any other hand. The diary of Lucas Rem survives, a German merchant who went to Venice in the very early sixteenth century to learn 'reckoning'. In his day's equivalent of the Harvard Business School, 'I learned reckoning full well in five-and-a-half months,' '*da lernte ich rechnen in fuenfeinhalb monat gar aus.*'

Between the ninth and the eleventh century, the business of kings and high nobles was in the hands of clerics. They were the only segment of the population which was literate and which was capable of balancing receipts and expenditures. The Church was also the only institution which had any money. Until at least the fourteenth century, a merchant's own bookkeeping was on scraps of paper, in day-books or diaries – except in Venice, Florence and Genoa, where a rudimentary double-entry system had existed earlier, and even there, so far as records go, it was used by only one or two merchant houses. A cleric, Fra Luca Pacioli, published a simple double-entry method of bookkeeping in 1494. Balance sheets were not in use until Simon Stevin, a Dutchman, described their uses in 1608. And only in 1673, the Frenchman, Jacques Savary, included inventory accounting in *The Complete Merchant, Le Parfait négociant*.

In a world where precision in the conduct of business was almost impossible, business remained a very private occupation. It had to rely more on honest faces than on accurate figures. Partnerships, of course, had to render accounts to partners, but the precision of such returns was based more on the confidence of man in man than on science. Even more than today, a man could cheat another only once, and the other had to learn his lesson without constant recourse to judges and to laws.

The agricultural and feudal economy of the Dark and Middle Ages could not conceive of trade as an independent pursuit. Every man was another's servant or bound to another by shared servitude. Life was lived in community and not in privacy. Work was done in community and not in privacy, and work was for sustenance not accumulation. The little that was made at all, was made within each large estate: clothes, the grinding of grain, and tools. Such goods and services were sold by the estate in its *gynaeceas* to its own residents – just as they were much later to be sold under the truck system at owners' 'tommy-shops'. The arbitrariness of princes was held in perilous check by settled relationships, custom, the bureaucracy of clerics and teachings of the Church. The idea of liberty was as yet unborn.

The interweaving of rights and duties had one hallowed purpose: not to disturb the established way of life and common worship. It was the master's right to hold men in bondage. He had the right to punish. It was also his duty to protect. He had the duty to protect the consumer against the merchant, and thus, for instance, to grant the common buyer a right of cavil, whereby the consumer could buy any part of the trader's goods without any right on the merchant's part to deny the purchase – either because it was too small, not fresh or because he would have to cut a whole to sell a part.

But his protection did not go far. Richard Winston[2] describes the extreme and oppressive taxation of the Middle Ages. Under Charlemagne, for example, the common man, freeman as well as serf, had to give at least three days in each week of his own labour to work his lord's land. This tax can be calculated: if the working week had six days, this tax alone represented a tax rate of 50 per cent. But in addition he had to pay his chevage (poll or property taxes) which had been customary west of the Rhine since Roman days. Then there were sales taxes, taxes on pasture and taxes in kind on owners or holders of manors and manses. There were *dona*, or traditional gifts to lords and stewards, from low to high. 'Gift' was a euphemism: these were compulsory donations. There were harbour fees, bridge tolls and market tolls as additional imposts on trader and peasant. And, of course, tax evasion led to heavy fines.

Beyond these burdens, dishonest officials demanded bribes. There was little redress for the victims of the feudal system; the official or lord who demanded money was also the one who heard the complaints of the oppressed in his own court of justice. The separation of executive and judiciary – that simple principle so indispensable for justice – did not exist. The only check on the rapacity of officials was the king himself, and the king could not be everywhere. Charlemagne tried to send out inspectors, *missi*, to check abuses. But it happened, and happened more than once, that the guardians of justice themselves became unjust and added to the burden.

When, in addition, the common man had to provide fodder and food as well as men – perhaps himself – for constant wars, the burdens were unbearable.

Nationhood had lesser meaning then than in later centuries or than it has today: the common man's medieval world meant fixed tenancy inside a global village under the Eternal Firmament. God was ever present; His spirit moved upon the face of the earth and the waters, immanent and awing. Heaven and earth were not just a spiritual, but a *physical* whole. The heavenly ranks described by St Jerome and St Ambrose, with their Seraphim and Cherubim, their Thrones, Dominions, Virtues, Powers, Principalities, Archangels and Angels, almost exactly mirrored the rankings of feudal precedence. (These, in their English form, are: Royal Princes, Royal Dukes, Dukes, Marquises, Earls, Viscounts, Barons, Baronets and Knights.)

Ordinary honesty, in a society so closely supervised, was not a subject of debate: the 'free' English tenant sokeman, the 'free' French alodiary, the less free villein and the unfree serf lived in honesty by rote. Knights favoured honour over honesty. They would rather fight with sword than pay their debts with money. The reasons why knights were held in greater esteem than merchants were, in Ruskin's words, two: because 'the former appear capable of self-sacrifice – the latter, not,' and because, while it does not appear reasonable that a peaceable and rational merchant should be held in less honour than one whose trade is slaying, nevertheless mankind has always given preference to the soldier: 'For the soldier's trade is not slaying, but being slain.'[3]

The knight preferred to be addressed as 'robust man' or 'vigorous man'. 'Man of honour' or 'honest man' was a second-class form of address for use by merchants. In the late Middle Ages, kings were worse than knights.

On the other hand, as Tawney[4] pointed out, if we insist on the prevalence of avarice and greed in high places, we ought also to admit that men had not learned to persuade themselves that greed was enterprise and avarice economy. Kings and nobles were defiant, but they were not hypocritical.

Notes

1 A. J. P. Taylor, 'The Turn of the Half-Century' (1950), in *Europe, Grandeur and Decline*, Penguin Books, London, 1967.
2 Richard Winston, *Charlemagne*, Eyre and Spottiswoode, London, 1956.
3 John Ruskin, 'The Roots of Honor', *Cornhill Magazine*, London, 1860.
4 R. H. Tawney, *Religion and the Rise of Capitalism*, John Murray, London, 1926/1944, p. 60.

8

Mercantilists and Adventurers

The Rise of Mercantilism

Mercantilism became the bracket between the village-based economy of the Middle Ages and our own times. Mercantilism's vestiges are still with us, just as the vestiges of medieval economic thought survived into the age of mercantilism.

Unlike the Middle Ages which considered exports an impoverishment, mercantilism considered imports an impoverishment. But in return for good gold bullion, exports were a blessing. This new view did not, of course, extend to the export of knowledge and skills. Venice confiscated the property of emigrant glassworkers. English statutes penalized the 'enticement of labourers' to go out of the kingdom. A French ordinance of 1682 imposed the death penalty on workers who left the kingdom. The morality of it was odd: skilled workers could immigrate into France and were made welcome, but if they tried to emigrate they were to be put to death. Such prohibitions on the loss of skills made sense by the logic of the age – as it still does in the Eastern Bloc of nations.

The feudal overlords of the Middle Ages had not been deeply patriotic. There was enough universalism in the Church, and enough had remained of the internationalism of the later Roman empire, to quash such ideas. Nationalism would have disturbed the stable and world-encompassing dominion of God. But between the fourteenth and the seventeenth century, the idea of kingship and of nationhood converged. The new principle that 'the King's faith is the people's faith' was extended to the economy: the king's trade became the merchants' trade – and vice versa. Change no longer held great terrors. With their hands tightly on the reins, kings ceased to fear a change of horse.

The Maintenance Economy, with great gaps remaining almost to this day, was yielding to an Exchange Economy. Before the twelfth century, the treasury of the kingdom had physically accompanied the king and his retinue in carts and ox-drawn wagons, but now no longer. Having hitherto been personal borrowers (and frequently personal defaulters), kings now began to lean on the institution of a national debt. This did not put an end to all defaults, but it was more than convenient to be able to pass debts from one's own royal person on to all the people. The king's income remained, but his own duty to repay debts was satisfactorily lessened.

Kings and merchants were united, at least by sentiment, in a spirit of patriotic royalism. It seemed right to find an identity between the private and the public interest. And, since the public interest became identified with the interests of the king, merchants also identified with him. Both did well from this. Kings became grander, merchants richer. By royal privilege, merchants also gained advantage over the merchants of other countries.

On behalf of king and country, colonies were sought. Colonies could, first, be robbed of their gold and silver; next, their cheap labour could be used; then, colonies would buy the products of the dominator; last, they would thereby be denied to other nations.

The Dutch East India Company, for instance, paid Indonesian pepper growers about one-tenth of its selling price in Holland. But it paid an annual 18 per cent dividend to its shareholders for 198 years – in addition to its payments of dues and taxes to the government. This astonishing return was made despite thefts by its officials and despite a great increase in its capital.

Seen purely as business, the discovery of America may have been an expensive mistake. Businessmen financed most conflicts, and their costs turned out to be higher than their returns. One historian[1] believes that the money helped to set Catholics against Lutherans, the house of Valois against the house of Hapsburg, the English against the Spanish, the Spanish against the Flemish, the Hanse against England, Portugal against the Arabs. And Braudel, the great French historian, notices that since the Spanish and Portuguese conquest, the Mediterranean Sea 'psychologically' still surrounds South America. But it has done little long-term good to either of these nations – so far.

Colonial policies went wrong in at least one other fateful case: North America. The American colonies refused to pay double damages – duties on their imports from Britain as well as taxes on their exports – and freed themselves of British rule.

Merchant-Adventurers: the Dutch

However protectionist, restrictive and nationally minded, the mercantilist state could not deny that the activities of merchants gave it its strength (or, had the word been in use then, ignore that 'mercantilism' derives from the Latin word for merchant). Its vigour lay in the growth of trade and of the means of trade: of merchant navies, merchant banking, buying and selling, mining, manufacturing, shipbuilding, fisheries. Armies, navies, the conquest of colonies, the establishment of state-owned industries, protected frontiers manned by excise men and customs agents – these and other expensive encumbrances were superimposed on business by the kings of nation-states; of England, Spain, France, Russia and the rest.

To be sure, not all trade was done in splendid domestic isolation. If nothing else, the demand for luxury clamoured for international trade. In one of his comedies, Ben Jonson (1572–1637) has an actor speak of dressing in a neck chain from Savoy, cuffs from Flanders, a Naples hat with its Roman hat band set with a Florentine agate, a sword made in Milan, a cloak from Geneva with fine buttons from Brabant, and gloves from Madrid.

At times called the Low Countries, at others the Netherlands and United Provinces, States-General or Dutch Republic, the part of them called Holland took a different path. They were not mercantilist in the same sense as were the kingdoms of France and Britain. In commercial spirit they had been Non-conformist even before the Reformation. They did not care for what was sacred to the state, but they cared a great deal for what filled their purses. Unlike the centralized kingdoms of France, Britain and Spain, the Dutch kept to a culture of cities and towns as islands free of feudalism and the absolute power of kings. In the seventeenth century, their Golden Age, six out of ten Dutchmen lived in cities. These cities did, of course, draw on the agricultural and other products of their own country, but they drew as easily on the products of Baltic countries, France, and the Dutch East Indies. They also traded African products – mostly slaves.

The Netherlands became a great trading republic, and Amsterdam, in the lifetime of Ben Jonson, grew to trading greatness on quite unmercantilist assumptions. Violet Barbour[2] describes how, suddenly, it seemed, the city was there, and in it a chamber of assurance in 1598; how the United East India Company was chartered in 1602; how a new bourse was begun in 1608 and in 1616 a special bourse for transactions in grain; how the exchange bank was founded in 1609 and a lending bank in 1614.

The Amsterdam of the mid-seventeenth century was free of the received ideas of mercantilism. All the world and all the world's goods were welcome there, to be sold freely and to be bought freely. Italian exchangers were to be seen; Venetians and Frenchmen came to invest in the West India Company; in mid-century, Florentines owned banks in the city; there were Tuscan shareholders in the East India Company; a company of Genoese merchants had a ship built in Amsterdam with which to trade to Portugal, Spain and the Mediterranean; Armenians displayed silks from Russia, Turkey, Persia and India. She shows how, between noon and one o'clock, Germans, Poles, Turks, even Hindus and other foreign peoples, jostled one another in a hubbub of bargaining.[3] She might have added Iberian Jews from Spain and Portugal, Flemings, French Huguenots and others.

Amsterdam was like an inverted Tower of Babel in which the confusion of tongues brought men together instead of putting them asunder. Amsterdam was a triumph of uninhibited trade, and of an infrastructure to support it.

Bullion and specie came from Spain; Italian bankers, Portuguese dealers and German merchants brought in more. In 1670 the Dutch had a merchant navy of about half a million tonnes, twice as many as Britain at the time. Even as late as 1790, long after they had lost their great ascendancy, their foreign trade per head of population (exports and imports) was over four times greater than Britain's, nearly eight times that of France, fourteen times Spain's, thirty-three times Italy's.

They were good bookkeepers; they had credit and deposit banking; their state debts were funded, not floating; they knew the measurement of time and its cost; they knew the techniques of foreign exchange; they knew paper credit in the form of merchants' notes (Bills of Exchange, Trade Bills and Fine Trade Bills); they issued receipts for bullion (Gold Certificates); receipts for merchandise stored in warehouses (Depositary Receipts); their in-and-out *entrepôt* trade in grain and other goods was the greatest in the world. They lived well, but well within their incomes; they were both careful *and* venturesome. In their day the three indispensables for national success coincided: high savings, high investment, high standards of skills and education.

They needed few laws against usury: their rates of interest were the lowest anywhere. They liked stability: Sidney Homer[4] tells us that, in 1624, Elsie, the daughter of George, invested 1,200 florins in the bonds of a Dutch company which had been chartered in 1323, and whose purpose was the repair of dykes. The company survived until at least 1957 and paid the interest on Elsie's bonds until then.

They were republicans. They had no kings nor any native nobility of the blood. True, they had an elite of burghers, stiff, conscious of their status. Their society was as stratified as any. But it was not divided into noble and ignoble ranks. Rather, it was divided into men of lesser station and men who had *earned* their higher station. Simon Schama[5] says that their commercial patricians failed to practise the thrift becoming to good Calvinists; their houses, he proves, were outwardly too fine and inside even finer. Their modesty, though they were anxious to be modest, was often ostentatious. But they were good Calvinists in one thing: they earned and reinvested their money with true Calvinistic professionalism and earnestness, unlike the sportsmen-nobles of France and England. They should, perhaps, be called a chrematocracy – the rule of merchants intent on making money; but one should not coin new words.

The Dutch held to their eminence from the sixteenth until the early eighteenth century when they declined through involuntary war, the rise of France and Britain, and heavy taxes. These, particularly internal taxes and excises to pay for defence, drove up their costs and wages.

Until then, theirs had been the first complete capitalist society and it had taught their more powerful and populous successors many lessons.

Notes

1 Miriam Beard, *A History of the Businessman*, Macmillan, New York, 1938, pp. 222–3.
2 Violet Barbour, *Capitalism in Amsterdam in the 17th Century*, Johns Hopkins Press, 1950, p. 17.
3 Ibid, pp. 56–7.
4 Sidney Homer *A History of Interest Rates*, Rutgers University Press, New Brunswick, NJ, 1963.
5 Simon Schama, *The Embarrassment of Riches: Dutch Culture in the Golden Age*, Knopf Inc., New York, and Collins, London, 1987, ch. 5.

9

Industry and Society

Gold and the Privilege of Kings

The vessels of colonial trading corporations plied from the ports of Holland, Britain and France, to India, the East and West Indies, and North and South America.

With equal legitimacy, slavers sailed to the plantations of the New World. In the eighteenth century, they plucked their human cargoes from Africa at an average rate of 55,000 per year – human cargoes that were soon to die for cotton, sugar and tobacco. One slave trading establishment, with the liberalism engendered by the Enlightenment, named its slave ships after the prophets and prophecies of human dignity: 'Voltaire', 'Rousseau', 'The Social Contract'.

'One who has gold,' observed Christopher Columbus, 'does as he wills in the world, and it even sends souls to Paradise.' In a little more than a century the Indian population was reduced by 90 per cent in Mexico (where the population fell from 25 million to 1.5 million), and by 95 per cent in Peru. They were slain in war, sent to Castile as slaves, or consumed in the mines and other labours . . . 'Who of those born in future generations will believe this? I myself who am writing this and saw it and know most about it can hardly believe that such was possible.'[1]

We note, incidentally, that Columbus, when setting out on his voyage, was to receive a 10 per cent commission on all gold and merchandise produced in consequence of his discoveries, as well as an option to buy a 12.5 per cent share of any ship subsequently setting out to trade.

Other ships sailed with less legitimacy: holders of Letters of Marque from one royal crown or another, pirates, corsairs, buccaneers, privateers, freebooters. The Amsterdam Insurance Company, an early capitalistic enterprise in the age of mercantilism, had to maintain sixty men-of-war to escort the ships it had insured.

It was an age of glitter and glory, an age of greed and the pursuit of gold. It was also an age of idle nobles and busy Nonconformist merchants – Puritans and Huguenots – whom we shall revisit.

History may or may not demonstrate in hindsight that mercantilists were wrong. Their belief that excess of coin or gold from foreign trade – 'much money . . . gotten yearly to make the happiness compleat' – was as wrong then for England, France and Spain, as it has turned out to be for Japan today. But what we now call adversarial competition was then the intellectual and practical norm. It protected native nascent industry and trade. Newly founded state and private factories, particularly in France, produced the fine tapestries and silks which made for jobs, for skills and for luxury. Being intended for the court and for the rich, standards were high and quality inspection strict. To improve manufacture, craftsmen were imported and techniques were bought – such as a method to make stockings 'ten times more quickly than with a needle'. Vagabonds and vagrants, the poor and indigent, were pressed into long hours of factory service or into the *corvée* of forced labour to build roads and bridges. This was done in order to teach lower orders the moral blessings of hard work. Moral blessings, that is to say, without financial blessings.

This, mark it, was nationalization by kings, not socialists. France, for one, had comparatively more state-owned industry then than she has had ever since. By Charles the Third's *Ordonnance sur la gendarmerie*, in 1439, a standing army, absent in Europe since the fall of Rome, made its reappearance. It needed standardized ammunition and supplies on a large scale – a ready-made large customer for the capitalism of mass production which was to follow.

No significant economic activity was legal by general or common law. Everything was by the privilege of the king and by special charter. None dared doubt that the king had the right to grant economic privileges. An edict by Henry IV of France, in 1603, similar to Louis XI's 137 years earlier, explains that arts and manufactures are to be encouraged as 'the sole means of avoiding the transport out of the kingdom of the precious metals and the consequent enrichment of our neighbours'. Monopoly was sometimes granted to private entrepreneurs, at others to the state itself. The French state has, for example, kept a monopoly on tobacco since 1674. Charters were given to found great colonizing companies. And, since the state had provided the endowment, the state also had the right of regulation.

The state regulated; it unified and centralized. The civil service grew. With it grew bureaucracy. The great Colbert, 1619–93, Minister of Finance to Louis XIV, found that in mid-century there were 45,780 offices in the justice and finance departments alone, of which he thought at least 40,000 were superfluous. Civil service appointments in France could be bought for money. At times, the income from such sales represented one-third of all her revenues.

The late eighteenth and early nineteenth centuries, the age of early capitalism, returned to a medieval view of the virtues of thrift and parsimony. It would not afford hospitals for the sick. It would not, from within, prevent the misery of children working in dark satanic mills. It would not resist the iniquities which resulted from David Ricardo's 'Iron Law of Wages' – the belief, namely, that higher wages would mean a larger population, but that a larger population would in turn mean lower wages. It chose to share Malthus's pessimism: 'At Nature's mighty feast there is no vacant cover for . . . a man who is born into a world already possessed [by others].'[2]

Early capitalism was an age of strict reason, but little reasonableness, and, as usual, the more there was of reason, the less there was of reasonableness. Both the Middle Ages and the early capitalist period agreed with the words of the Saviour that 'the poor will always be with you.' But there was a difference: the medieval world had explained the existence of beggars by the working of God's mysterious will. The nineteenth century explained that beggars existed by the working of inexorable economic laws.

Yet again, another age begat a faultless logic to justify its moral ambiguities, and, as always, fat sanctimony was lighting candles to pretended virtues. Perhaps the most hopeful sign that we live in a better age is our incipient belief that poverty is not the rule but a difficult exception.

The Age of Steam

Capitalism had no sudden beginnings. Large, classically capitalistic industries had existed long before the early nineteenth century –

privately owned, or properties of kings, or of alliances, in one form or another, of merchants with princes.

The textile industry of Florence in the fourteenth century, for example, had been heavily mechanized, though driven by water power. It had also been well capitalized: Florence was a centre of banking. In 1341, Alidosi reported that there were great machines in Florence, which moved by the waters of the Arno, swiftly spun and threw 4,000 threads of silk, performing in an instant the work of 4,000 women spinners. By 1371, Alidosi listed thirteen mills of similar efficiency in Florence.

The ringing of a bell summoned and released the workers, whose number in Florence was in the tens of thousands. They had no right of union or, for that matter, any other rights. Supervised by mighty foremen, production in the textile industry passed through some thirty specialized stages, in which each worker had but one task to perform. Similarly, English cloth factories, using only water power but many newly invented machines, had also grown to importance before the age of steam.

In Luebeck, by the end of the same fourteenth century, the making of rosaries was no longer on a handicraft basis; it had gone over to the 'putting-out' system. Small capitalists supplied funds and materials to poor families who were paid scant wages for the work. Miriam Beard comments on the curious circumstance that modern industrial capitalism, while destroying medieval religious values, should burst through in the mass production of prayer beads.

'Putting-out' has a long and continuous history. The town of Solingen in Germany was an example. It manufactured cutlery and hardware, and still does. There, much of the work was done in *Kotten*, or cottages, where a family would add this or that finish to the piece and then return it to the blanking forge for sale. This division of work was continuous from Solingen's beginnings as a sword-making centre in the Dark and Middle Ages before the year 1000. People there still talk of these 'cottages' from living memory.

It was a system of many abuses. In the middle of the sixteenth century, an English law proclaimed that 'rich clothiers do oppress the weavers . . . by engrossing [monopolizing] of looms into their hands and letting them out at . . . unreasonable rents.' Such were the harsh origins of the 'buy-and-lease-back' method of financing machinery and plant.

The time had come for merchants to slough off the royal shackles, to be left alone and be *laissez-faire* to engage in foreign and domestic trade. Mercantilism's role was mainly done; supplicating for the king's leave was turning burdensome.

Man and Machine

There is a natural tendency in people to believe that the things they hold good must be connected with each other, that what happens to be together, belongs together.

Thus we, like Goethe, may believe that the operation of the market furthers both the creation of wealth and the brotherhood of man. Or we may believe that business has a natural affinity with the humanities in the pursuit of a good world. It is desirable but it is not so. Business often leads to cooperation but it does not create brotherhood. Still, we must welcome even this small mercy. As to the humanities, they and business coexist but live in separate worlds and only meet by special assignation.

The nineteenth century threw everything open to change, including human relationships. It reinforced the division of the population into classes and it sharpened class-consciousness. But economic circumstances alone do not create a class ideology. By itself, rich or poor, condition is not class. The working people of the nineteenth century were not inclined to political or economic theorizing. Essentially, their moral outlook was bound to old archetypes: 'the golden rule', simple moral outrage, the cry for rights and fairness.

But no balance could be found: the relentless acquisition of wealth which the middle classes saw as just was hateful to the poor. Not wealth or lack of wealth alone but the goading mastery of some and the impotent dependency of others made classes; not in North America, but in Britain In North America, all European immigrants felt, and were, liberated. In Britain there could not be any such release, nor any sense of liberation.

Business itself worked incessantly as if no other destiny existed. Yet just such concentration on its work abetted a new destiny. Not only business but also government acquired a new conception of property. To the Middle Ages and the age of mercantilism property had been tangible things – things that do not beget other things: land, gold, treasure, saintly relics. Now, however, money and property came to be seen as a protean, fertile and begetting seed; money could make money could make money.

To business, property was a right to make their money work; to government, it meant colonial development.

But colonial administration was, in a sense, a property of the upper and the middle classes. The upper class furnished viceroys, governors-general, governors and generals; the middle class supplied the staffs of colonial bureaucracy. For the middle class particularly, colonies were a source of superior jobs. They offered it additional employment and allowed it to become more numerous. In Britain, a new kind of private school, the 'public' school, educated some clever boys to become platonic guardians of the heathen. It also produced many asses to carry the White Man's Burden.

At home, bureaucracy had its own two forms of property. The first was custody of the nation's affairs. The second was, needless to say, its own perpetuation. It had outgrown what Max Weber called its 'patrimonial' functions. It now became the guardian of legality, and, in time, it tended to define legality. This was so particularly in France with her old tradition of centralized government, and in Prussia with her new fashion in political philosophy.

Love of country, love of soil, love of motherland or fatherland (depending on one's nationality), love of flag, dislike of the flags of other nations, were all conflated into one strong sense of statehood and a desire for national aggrandizement. In 1871, Bismarck had proclaimed that colonies for Germany were as unsuitable as a silk-and-sable coat for a poor shirtless Polish nobleman, but a few years later he turned his own coat and proclaimed that German civilization was good for German colonies. And vice versa, one may presume.

According to the Oxford English Dictionary, the first recorded use of the word 'nationalism' in its present sense was in 1853. As the culture of each nation was buffetted by its own mixing of these elements, so each nation became, first, distinctively acculturated and, next, inimical to its neighbours.

From this arose a natural morality more self-righteous than meticulous, more patriotically boastful than appreciative of the talents of other nations, more narcissistic than universal. Nations failed to remind themselves that Narcissus had been one of the world's most fatal lovers.

Cant was unquestionably sincere: 'The authority of the British Crown is at the moment [1853] the most powerful instrument, under

Providence, of maintaining peace and order in many extensive regions of the earth, and thereby assists in diffusing among millions of the human race, the blessings of Christianity and civilization,' said a British statesman – and himself believed it.

There was, amid the smoke and thrust, a great deal of enlightenment in the age, but also a great deal of obfuscation; much sincerity and much hypocrisy; much church attendance, but too little Christian humility and social intention; much gold, too little guilt; many grand hotels and many more hovels; much wisdom and much posturing; many reasonable men and many silly. Its creations were miraculous; its destructions were egregious. To it we owe free trade and the foundations of the world's present science and wealth, but also the wars and revolutions of this century.

For most of its civilized history mankind has lived in a condition of overpopulation – overpopulation being a count of heads compared with inadequate resources to sustain them.

Norbert Elias[3] explained that in a heavily industrialized society with intensive utilization of the land and with highly developed long-distance trade, a large number of people can live more or less tolerably. But in a medieval barter economy, for example, with extensive agricultural methods and little long-distance trade, this meant overpopulation. In this sense, Europe in the Middle Ages was overpopulated: there was 'no land [left free] without a lord'.

One symptom of overpopulation, incidentally, was the emergence of a sizeable class of younger sons of landed lords, deprived of land of their own, who now became a medieval class of European samurai longing for soil to conquer. They furnished some manpower and incentives for the Crusades.

From the Middle Ages until the age of the Industrial Revolution other physical constraints made unlimited growth impossible and unimaginable. There was not enough energy and public hygiene. Transport was expensive, land was possessed by incumbent owners, there was little science and not enough technology. These were the constraints for most of the aeons before the Industrial Revolution.

This present age is the only we have ever known in which unlimited growth has been a realistic vision. The world found its unfoldment. Ideologies grew which took boundlessness for granted: the Inevitability of Progress, the Perfectibility of Man, Popular Democracy, the Pursuit of Happiness, Marxism, Socialism, Free Enterprise, Free

Trade. The endlessness of the human imagination was unconfined by finitudes. Things came our way. We saw our own nature – human weakness and inconstancy – as the only remaining constraint to an eternity of possibilities. And, to adapt a phrase of R. H. Tawney, at the same time as the modern temper took our destinations for granted, it grew enthralled by the hum of the engines.[4]

Beyond, in the future, probably, undoubtedly, lie other constraints. The sponge of nature will no longer absorb the leavings of uncountable mankind. Civilization may find the means to overcome the limits of global physics and chemistry, or it may not. But for the present, in this wedge of time between impossibilities, we (in the West, at least) live in the Era of Great Comfort.

Notes

1 Michel Beaud, *A History of Capitalism 1500–1980*, Macmillan, London, 1984, p. 19.
2 T. R. Malthus, *Essay on the Principle of Population*, 1803 edn. London, pp. 531–2. (Not included in the 1826 edition.)
3 Norbert Elias, *Power and Civility*, Basil Blackwell, Oxford, 1982, p. 35.
4 R. H. Tawney, *Religion and the Rise of Capitalism*, John Murray, London, 1926/1944, p. 19.

Section 4

Ideas that Shaped Business

Preamble

Acton, the historian, advised us to study problems, not periods, and we shall follow this advice. Section 4 sketches the development of certain moral and practical ideas in history from the Middle Ages to the rise of capitalism, taking the idea of interest (or usury) as its theme. It touches upon the role of 'outsiders': the Nonconformists. The next section, section 5, will speak of two other very different 'nonconformists': the Jews and the Japanese.

Usury has been the subject of centuries-long debate. It involved commerce, church and state. The fate of this concept demonstrates how every idea suffers from some unforgiving reality, and how every reality suffers from some unforgiving idea. This is one theme of this section.

The other is the development of the rationale of business.

The Church's doctrine of usury, in the Middle Ages and for centuries thereafter, forbade the taking of interest, whether from a neighbour or from a stranger. This meant that it was also forbidden to make direct or indirect charges for the administrative cost incurred in lending. It meant that credit given would yield nothing; indeed, when overhead costs were considered, it would yield only losses – less than nothing. It meant that one could not compare transactions. One deal could not, in profitability and economic efficiency, be weighed against another. It meant that the cost of time used in the transfer of money from one town to another, from one country to another, could not be invoiced, and hence it meant that money could not be transferred without loss. It meant that a lender could not charge reimbursement for insurance against a borrower's default. It meant that, when lending, no correction could be made to take account of inflation and different degrees of risk: a zero rate of interest could be neither multiplied nor divided. In short, it meant that business and money had no rationale and could not settle. The Church's admirable universalism was irreconcilable with any business universalism – even with an honest business universalism.

Since some honour was necessary, commerce devised its own forms of it – deviously at times. It was not, however, a code that the Church could approve. It came from practice. The daily practices of commerce refined the notions of what is an asset and what is a liability. Businessmen constantly honed their decisions in terms of money: what is mine and what is yours; how much is mine and how much yours; how much should be mine and how much yours; how much is mine today and yours tomorrow. If they succeeded, it was because money is the only commodity that has quantity only and no qualities.

10

Christianity and Enterprise

The Idea of Work

Work implies transformation. Therefore, ages of ferment, societies of becoming, have generally praised work, whereas static societies, societies of being, have regarded work as interference with dignity.

With one or two doubtful exceptions, the Greeks, in whose world slaves performed the manual labour, believed that work coarsens the human spirit; that it interferes with the contemplation of virtue; that it is inimical to perfect changelessness; that it hinders the achievement of high-minded equanimity.

The Children of Israel maintained that Adam lost the Garden of Eden by his own sin. Henceforward man must earn his bread by the sweat of his brow. Work is punishment. The Promised Land, with its prospect of a flush of milk and honey without the need to pump, is a reward. In addition, money gained by work only fills the stomach, but God feeds the soul. 'Labour not to be rich; cease from thine own wisdom' (Proverbs 23:4).

Similarly, early and medieval Christians believed with Matthew (6:32–4) that God knows our needs and that if we first seek His kingdom and righteousness all these things will be added to us. We need take no thought for tomorrow; it will take care of itself. Work, medieval man held, is for sustenance; it is a means for the remedy of sins; it is there to provide money for charity. If we must work it is because every age is the purgatory of the next age. There was, of course, St Paul who said that if any would not work, neither should he eat. But why did he say it? Not because work is good in itself, but only so that a man might eat his own bread 'in quietness' and not be a burden on others.

In the context of the life of the Middle Ages, St Paul's admonition was superfluous. With work, there was little enough to eat; without work there was nothing. In St Matthew there was at least hope. In St Paul there was no practical relevance.

Medieval feudal lords, meanwhile, in a world which was ordained for ever and sustained by serfs, saw the Cross more in the hilt of their swords than in the calloused hands of the Carpenter.

With the Renaissance, with such as Leonardo da Vinci, came the ferment that changed the attitude to work. There was now a distinction between God's created nature and man's creative nature. Then with Luther came the idea of work as worship. With Calvin and the Puritans came the idea that success in business and earthly endeavours is proof of election by God. Later, in the eighteenth century, came fascination with worker-machines. With Locke and Adam Smith came the foundations of economics, which is, after all, the science of work and its effects.

We have today arrived at the point at which we speak of a 'right to work'. Work is now man's blessing instead of man's curse. The demand for a right to work is a demand for the right to dividends from each man's capital: his ability to work.

But if it is a right, it is a right that has as yet not been explicitly recognized by any Western government, and what it has become in communist countries is mentioned below. Nor is it likely to be recognized in the foreseeable future, because labour power is everywhere treated as a commodity rather than as capital.

Whether it is capital or a commodity depends on the answer to some questions. Is it property in the sense in which patents and copyrights, or personal rights and freedoms, are a property? If the answer is yes, then we have to ask further questions. Is labour power divisible into degrees and categories? Is all labour power, even unskilled, an inherent property and capital of man? Or do skills and experience make it such? Or high intelligence? Or degrees of energy and creativity?

Or must we discard altogether the idea that the ability to work is property and a form of capital? Do we discard the concept of man's 'bundle of powers' and judge the tree by its 'bundle of fruits', as we do now?

These questions must be asked, but remain unanswered here. And the reason why they cannot be answered now is that, in essence, they are an argument about the dignity of man, rather than about man's rights – about what man is, as against what he can do. Whether a claim for dignity will translate into a legal right depends on the prevailing social philosophy and the mood of voters and legislatures. It is, at any rate, an old argument. Adam Smith made it more than 200 years ago in *The Wealth of Nations*, when he said that the property which every man has in his own labour, like the foundation of all property, is most sacred and inviolable.

The argument hovers between being a demand and a presumption. Other similar claims are already being fought in US courts, such as that dismissal from a job without due process is a violation of property rights. Dismissals without good cause are legally contestable in many other countries of Europe and elsewhere, but without, as in Anglo-Saxon law, being defined as infringements of *property* rights.

So far as business is concerned, the problem will not vanish just because no resolution is in sight. The problem is not academic, nor is it trivial. If one considers it, the argument that man's inner potential is a form of capital has been at the heart of all humanism and democracy: the argument being that, if a society is valuable, then its value must be at least equal to the sum of its parts. And since we believe in the sovereignty of the nation, we can hardly deny a degree of sovereignty to its parts, its members: because to deny it is to say that the sum of nothing is itself more than nothing. Paradoxically, our Western 'materialism', by endowing people with a small estate of their own, a house and garden, a testament and burial plot, civil standing and rank in some civic enterprise, with middle-classness, also endows them with the 'soul' of a somebody.

Equally paradoxically, in our society, which is based on an assumed value of the individual, the argument for a right to work carries greater weight than in collectivist societies.

Communist societies claim that they have recognized the right to work. They claim that none is unemployed – which is questionable. They demand that none be allowed unemployment – which is unquestionable. But compulsory work is a duty to work, and not a right to work. The one has been turned into the other, and, yet again, a personal capital has been turned into a public possession.

Marx wrote about 'surplus value'. He meant that all value is the result of work. The capitalist employer pays the worker less than the value he produces and keeps the surplus for himself as profit. He said that in future socialist economies workers may receive 'from the social supply of [the] means of consumption a share corresponding to their labour time'.[1]

It never came about. Workers under communism receive only a small part of the surplus value they produce. Instead, they receive what remains after the state has taken what it needs. It is the same principle as that on which children receive pocket money: from whatever is left that has not been allocated by their parents for other purposes. Everyone's surplus value has been appropriated by the state and everybody's labour is a national and not a private resource. A Chinese acquaintance who worked in a foreign joint-venture organization in China itself, related that the Chinese government charged the foreign partner company about 1,200 dollars per month for his services but paid him only 60. He received 5 per cent for his labour and the state took the 95 remaining per cent of 'surplus'.

Give or take a little, this method has remained in other Eastern Bloc countries, as, for example, when hiring a Rumanian secretary for the representative office of a foreign firm in Bucharest, or local assistants for a foreign embassy in any of these countries. The new foreign investment laws of the USSR have so far been tending in the same direction. If, indeed, the new foreign investment laws of communist countries prove to be ineffective, it will be because of their 'capitalistic' exploitation of the 'surplus' of their citizens – blatant enough to be resented by a foreign investor.

The Idea of Rational Speculation

From this digression on work we are led into the essence of business: return on money capital, return on invested capital and the notion of interest.

There are many views on what made capitalism possible, and when it became possible: historical views, sociological views, theories of classes, theories of technological advance, development theories, theories of religion, of changes in historical consciousness, of achievements by powerful or charismatic men.

It cannot even be certain that the twin capitalism we know today, industrial capitalism, was not coincidental. What is certain is that capitalism started from trade. The need to trade and exchange made money necessary. Banking started from trade, so did non-military shipping and transport. The need to complete the chain of trade by what we would today call vertical integration, drew business, often unwillingly, into mining, smelting and manufacturing. The brilliant mechanical inventions of Leonardo da Vinci were in his day used for war, not factories.

It happened that a crop of engineer-entrepreneurs arose in the mid-eighteenth century, who, like Edison in the twentieth, fused the idea of industry and technology indissolubly with capitalistic enterprise. In truth, industry arose more as an adjunct of capitalism than as the core which it is today.

But to a businessman there is a prior and indispensable condition without which capitalism would be impossible: the possibility of rational speculation, of measurable risk.

Rational speculation only becomes possible when all potential investments are set in one calculable frame of comparison. It is the framework of time in which profits from the investment of money in trade or industry on the one hand can be compared with the yield from financial investments and savings on the other. One then has a framework for the equivalence or non-equivalence of manufacturing and trading profits as against the return on money by way of interest. One then has a frame of time preference for investment now or later, in this or in that. It is then possible to gauge the cost of one business opportunity against the cost of another business opportunity.

Whenever and wherever this conjunction happened, capitalism was ready to be born. Money and gold ceased to be a barren hoard and became productive savings.

It was a long road, because, while profits were always permitted within reason, interest, the missing link of rational business, was not. We shall follow the road.

The Idea of Usury

'To thy brother thou shalt not lend upon usury.' This part of a sentence from Deuteronomy (23:20) concerning the charging of interest was the curb under which all business was to be conducted until quite recently. 'Was to be', rather than always was. 'Recently', too, must be defined: it may mean any time between the twelfth and nineteenth century, depending on the country, the temporal rulers, the doctrine of the Roman and other churches at the time, their broad or narrowmindedness at the time, and the financial needs of throne and altar.

Christian Byzantium, the Eastern Roman empire, for example,

rarely enforced the absolute prohibition on the taking of interest. It continued an earlier Roman tradition of regulated interest rates but did not deny the need for interest as a whole.

The logic of the case against the taking of interest has suffered a curious inversion over the centuries. The ancient Christian logic was that interest is unreasonable, for why should the passive lender benefit from the exertions of the active borrower? In R. H. Tawney's summary, to take usury was contrary to Scripture; it was contrary to Aristotle; it was contrary to nature, for it was to live without labour; it was to sell time which belongs to God for the advantage of wicked men; it was to rob the borrower, to whom, since he made it profitable, the profits should belong.[2]

The view that the taking of interest on borrowed money is unreasonable has changed; today, *not* to take interest is unreasonable. Not only is it unreasonable, it is foolish and wrong. 'What man,' in the words of Thomas Wilson in the sixteenth century, 'is so madde [as] to deliver his moneye out of his owne possession for naught . . . whoe is he that will not make of his owne the best he can?'

Moreover, the belief that no one would even think of lending money without charging interest, has become official government doctrine. Most forms of corporate interest-free loans are not acceptable to government revenue services. They impute interest even where none has been charged and require income tax to be paid on such putative interest even though there was no income.

What, in the medieval view, was all right, and what was not?

Charging rent for land was all right because land yields 'the bounties of nature' to him who rents it.

Annuities in their medieval and early Renaissance forms, (often called 'census' or *rentes*), were generally all right for similar reasons: the gain from them was not certain but conditional on the times. A census was then considered more a mortgage on a fruitful property like an estate or farm. A farm, after all, benefited from the bounty of nature, or suffered from its whims. In any case, many of these *rentes*, some in the nature of forced loans, were devices by governments to raise money by means other than straightforward taxation; hence, being a sort of tax, they could not be called usurious in the private sense.

Partnerships were all right because one joined a partnership for better or for worse, 'to gain or to lose'.

Penalties for the tardy repayment of loans were all right because the lender who received repayment of his money too late may have had to forgo an opportunity to make his own profit from it. (Mark this loophole, which was well exploited.)

What was not all right was pure interest, or, as the Church would put it, 'the sale of time itself'. She objected to the 'gain certain' of a loan, because interest was payable regardless of the risks the borrower may have had to take. And, whether the gain was from a loan at interest, or from any deal of the same or similar kind, it was 'filthy lucre'. Lend, said Christ, but do not hope to gain thereby – *date mutuo, nihil inde sperantes*.

Missing Links of Rationality

1   The misunderstanding of the nature of interest

The Church did not recognize the risks of a borrower's default to the lender. She did not recognize the existence of what we today call overhead costs. She did not take account of the erosions of inflation.

Had it been noticed that the value of a lent-out principal sum had sometimes shrunk in purchasing power during the time of the loan, the Church – foolish sometimes, but not uncharitable or wilfully unfair – would have upheld Deuteronomy in altered form; she would have permitted some adjustment to allow the lender to recover the par value of his loan. But the Church did not notice.

Inflation certainly existed: coin was clipped, bad money drove out good money, new coinage of lesser metal content was issued by kings to repay in cheap coin a debt incurred in good coin – and thereby cheat the lender. The price of gold fluctuated around the price of silver. There were other examples: in the late eighth-century Charlemagne twice vanquished Pannonia, the country of the Avars or Huns – later to become Hungary, the country of the Magyars. On the first occasion, the huge captured treasure was carried off to his Frankish kingdom in fifteen wagons – Byzantine coin, swords, cups, jewels, clasps, silks. This injection of precious metals inflated prices in Charlemagne's empire from walk to trot. 'The memory of man,' says Charlemagne's friend and chronicler Einhard, 'cannot recall any war by which [the Franks] . . . who hitherto had seemed almost paupers . . . were so enriched.' Shortly after the first came a second raid on the Avars. Another large trove was discovered. This too was carried off. Coming on top of the first inflation, this new injection of money caused prices to break into a canter if not gallop.

The phenomenon of inflation was simply too complicated to be included in a reckoning. The idea that things could become dearer because money had become cheaper, or that the velocity of circulation of money was affected by variations in its quantity, was quite beyond the compass of the canonical mind.

Lastly, gold and silver were seen as repositories of permanent, inherent and invariant value. This, in an ancient world, must not be thought strange, because the world of the Middle Ages was filled with inherent and invariant values: God, His word, the heavenly spheres, the crystal empyrean, the perfection of circles, damnation and redemption, lord and vassal, the Church. Imperishable gold and its cousin silver must be the divinely appointed yardsticks of all worldly values. It is an ineradicable belief still held today by insecure economists.

In the late fifteenth and in the sixteenth century, Europeans became aware of gross inflation. But, though the fact of inflation stared them in the face, the connection between inflation and the quantity of gold and silver did not become obvious to them. It was not until the early seventeenth century that Thomas Mun, in *England's Treasure by Fforraign Trade*, was to say that 'plenty of money in a kingdom doth make the native commodities dearer.'

Much gold and silver had arrived from the Americas. In 1493, the stock of gold had been about 550 tonnes; at the end of the sixteenth century, according to Braudel, it was 5,000 tonnes. Silver went from 7,000 to 60,000 tonnes. The cost of living rose from two to over sixfold.

There were other factors. Nevertheless, Luigi Enaudi estimated that in France, of the price increase of over six hundred per cent between 1471 and 1598, nearly half was attributable to the influx of precious metals. Braudel also tells us that, of the two learned men who in 1557 and 1558 surmised that there was a connection between new metal and inflation, one was not published for thirty-two years, the other not until 1912 – too late, one must suspect, to have been of cautionary value.[3]

2   From brotherhood to otherhood

The full sentence in Deuteronomy reads: 'Unto a stranger thou mayest lend upon usury; but to thy brother thou shalt not lend upon usury.'

The medieval church could have defined some men as 'strangers' as easily as define them all as 'brothers'. It is admirable that she chose to define them all as brothers. Not only did this represent an encompassing universalism, but one that encompassed in brotherhood. 'Medieval Christianity, aspiring to universalism . . . proposed to transcend the morality of clan by joining the "other" to the "brother".'[4]

But since such well-meaning universalism was not rational, it did not work too well. And so, ultimately, the universalism of brotherhood was replaced by rationality, the rationality which exists today. 'Brotherhood' has yielded to the prudent suspicions and careful credit checks of modern business. Toward buyers and sellers; toward borrowers and lenders, insurers, insured; towards shippers, consignors, consignees, warehousers; in short, towards everyone, business applied an evenhanded universalism, just as the Church did. But the one great difference is that our universalism treats *nobody* as brother. We are joined in a unity of universal wariness. Otherhood is automatic; brotherhood comes only after long acquaintance and within appropriate limits.

The official stand of the Church of the Middle Ages was admirable, but a little absurd. Who was there to make a loan without interest? A charitable neighbour, perhaps, a 'Joseph of the countryside who keeps the poor from starving'? There were, indeed, more than a few of these friendly Josephs. Small charity abounded in every corner of the Christian world. But it was a minor coin of life.

Larger coin was not lent from kindliness. Popes, kings, and princes borrowed from rich bankers outside the usual rules of damnation. Pope Innocent IV, in 1248, with Christian sufferance lightly tinted by the colour of necessity, even accepted some of these money-lenders as his 'peculiar sons' – *ecclesiae filii speciales*.

Evasion, 'chevisance', abounded. Contracts were drawn to conceal the nature of a deal; loans were dressed up as sales; advance deposits were taken prior to the loan as prepayment of interest; imaginary partnerships were formed; false invoices were rendered for pretended goods; invoices were issued at higher than real price; other 'neat tricks' of conversion of goods and money still familiar today were used; and, nearly always, some remuneration equivalent to interest, also known as usury, was exacted. With a little effort at hypocrisy one could, as did the sixteenth-century Genoese banker Lazaro Doria, assuage one's own 'pricklesome conscience'. Doria would not charge any interest on his own money. But when he lent money out, it somehow happened never to be his own.

Henry Pirenne explains how, in documents intended for the public, the reality was dissimulated. The borrower habitually agreed to repay, on the expiration of the term, a sum greater than that which he had in fact received; the difference formed the interest. Interest was forbidden; but as we have noted, damages for late repayment were permitted. And so, in loans with damages (*ad manaium*), the debt officially acknowledged is exactly that originally contracted. But on the nominal day of repayment the damages are paid, and at the same time the debt is renewed. It must have been understood that the debtor would not pay up on the agreed date, so that usury, like Shylock's 'merry bond', was here concealed under the guise of a penalty for delay.[5]

Or consider the Florentine *barratto*, a type of transaction frequently used in the later centuries of the Middle Ages. A *barratto* transaction might involve the sale of some commodity, say silk, at a nominal cash price of, say, 100. Its actual price with payment deferred by an agreed term of months, and including interest, might be 110. But it would not be repaid in cash; instead the buyer would pay part of it in, say, woollens on similar terms, and pay the balance in cash; or not pay the balance in cash, but instead in some velvet – again on similar terms. The transaction became impenetrable. Its justice or injustice could neither be proved nor disproved, and even though it clearly involved usury, the usury was veiled, obscured and secret.

In any case, the high finance of international banking of the day – lenders to cities and towns and, above all, to kings and princes, to bishops and popes at the summit of the feudal chain – was exempt, whereas Jews, the small fry of the credit world, were less exempt; they were the retailers of the usury business.

Such was the world in which the Church – defined in the Nicene Creed of 325 AD as 'one, holy, catholic and apostolic' – was not just one society within society at large, but the encompassing girdle of society. It was, of course, a world of unresolved contradictions. But if we today contentedly maintain that the virtues of democratic liberality are superior to the baleful darkness of dictatorship, we had better remember that for the whole of the millennium which comprises the Dark and Middle Ages, the very practices that we condemn today were the rules under which men then lived: absolutism; intolerance of dissent; the trammelling of trade; regulation of income and of spending; supervision of private morals; price controls and credit controls; punishments and servitudes; excommunication; unquestioning obedience to authority – all in the name of, and for the glory of, an unchangeable, highly articulated and protected doctrine.

We were until recently still neighbours of a particular variant of mediaevalism. It was the theistic mediaevalism of an all-encompassing doctrine that brooked no divorce between social policy and personal conduct; a medievalism in which the domination of a creed prevailed over any common desire; the mediaevalism of a god-idea which outvoted any majority. We refer, of course, to the worlds behind the Iron Curtain before Gorbachev. The curtain was not a curtain of iron, but a curtain of time.

But to those who hope that the Soviet Union's present leader may return his country to openness and transparency, one is obliged to point out that the Middle Ages were followed by mercantilism.

3 The redefinition of usury

With trade being done before the portals of cathedrals, churchmen had to reconsider the norms of trade in more systematic fashion. Was usury perhaps not wrong in every case, not always wrong, not wrong in all forms, not wrong from all – *neque passim, neque semper, neque omnia, neque ab omnibus*?

Some of them may have recalled St Ambrose's much earlier pronouncement (which certainly implied no acceptance of universal brotherhood) that a stranger was an enemy whom one could not easily conquer in war. On him 'you can quickly take vengeance with the hundredth', that is, by charging him interest. (Note that this is the first recorded example of 'salami tactics' for use against an enemy.)

St Bernardino of Siena (1380–1444) echoed the Ambrosian doctrine. He repeated that in the case of God's enemies, usury was lawful – if done not for the sake of gain but for the sake of the Faith. The motive was to be 'brotherly love'. In the first place, making the enemy poor by charging him interest weakened him, so that, in his despair, he might return to God. Furthermore, since he was a rebel against the true Faith, his goods did not belong to him anyway. In other words, good faith is not owed to him who breaks the Faith –

fides non servanda est ei qui frangit fidem. Strange are the ways of holiness!

Regarded thus, discrimination between brothers and others crept into the universalism of brotherhood. Given human nature, it was only a matter of time before the definition of 'others' was to be extended – at the expense of 'brothers'. The task, about two centuries later, would be Calvin's.

And so, beyond public definition there was private doubt and ecclesiastical debate. The banker of the Roman Church was Florence, where spinning and weaving had become an industry in the thirteenth century. Florentine trade was vigorous and its habits pagan. St Antoninus, its archbishop from 1446, was able to look soberly at the scene before him and conclude that there would be a great deal of harm done if there were no money that could be borrowed, but that few 'would offer to lend money unless they could get some profit by it'. He made a distinction between money employed as capital (and used the word in its modern sense) as distinct from current cash. If a merchant sustained a loss, who might otherwise have put his money into another commercial enterprise, he should be lawfully compensated by some form of interest.

The matter was now carefully analysed. Commercial realities now received elaborate Latin names: money loaned at risk of loss became *damnum emergens*; loss of profit a *lucrum cessans*; capital risk became a *periculum sortis*; and in all these cases the compensation called interest, *interesse*, became permissible within limits – as opposed to usury, *faeneratio* and *usura*, which was not. Consciences were mollified by definitions. Here also, and for the first time, we find the idea of compensation for the diversion of one business opportunity to another – 'opportunity cost' as we would call it now.

Work, too, received an altered definition by Antoninus. From having been man's curse, it now became 'his duty, his perfection and his happiness'. Antoninus[6] also distinguished between commercial (use) value, and 'eternal' (natural) value. As a living thing, he said, a mouse has of itself a higher value than dead wheat, yet to men it was of much lesser value.

4 The discovery of overhead costs

After this hedged and guarded recognition that interest was not always sinful, and that the work of merchants was not all tricks and usury, another element of the cost of doing business – hitherto hidden or ignored – was unveiled by an unexpected source. It was overhead costs, management costs, administrative costs.

According to Sidney Homer,[7] fifteenth-century Italian interest rates for short- and long-term loans to commercial establishments and governments hovered between 5 and 10 per cent. They were from 10 to 100 per cent to unreliable princes who were unable to offer adequate security. And the pawnshop lending rate to private borrowers was from 32.5 to 43.5 per cent, although officially limited to a maximum of 20.

In one of the cities of Italy, Perugia perhaps, a *mons pietatis*, or small-loans bank, was started in 1462 by Franciscans. The idea was born of charity. The purpose of the *monti* was to lend money to those whose only other recourse was pawnshops and usurers at outrageous rates. *Monti di pietà* spread to many other cities, including Venice. Another cleric, Bernardino of Feltre, pestered, preached and cajoled the authorities to deliver needy borrowers from having to pay over 30 per cent. He argued that they should pay only 5.

Still, that was 5 per cent more than the nothing-at-all prescribed by the prohibition against usury. Florence resisted: Bernardino was 'inconvenient and scandalous'. Augustinian and Dominican purists, too, being against interest in any form, agreed with Florence.

Here the usual dilemma of ethics was posed: what should happen when good principle is set against good principle? Should Deuteronomy remain, or was the command of Charity greater than Deuteronomy? Should poor but immortal souls be entitled to discounts on earth? Antoninus and charity prevailed; by 1493 even Florence opened shop.

Whether 5 per cent only, or sometimes 8, paying interest was still officially usury. And, therefore, equally officially, the 5 per cent was charged by the *monti* not as interest but as a 'cost-of-management charge' to defray the expenses of the operations.

By the beginning of the next century two popes had blessed the endeavours of the *monti*. Recognition of the reality of overhead costs – read 'usury' if you like, but do not speak it – thus came from the Church herself. She nodded in one eye and winked the other. The common belief that in trade a merchant's gross margin is also his net profit had been laid to rest.

'The Acres Melting'

In the Middle Ages there had been only one major class of literates – the priesthood. By the fifteenth century there were two: priesthood and merchants. One class read Aristotle in Latin, the other only read the figures in books of accounts. One tried to conserve, the other to revise. However cogent Aristotle, figures were more convincing still. The process was accelerated by the invention of Gutenberg's movable type and the production of paper for printing. Both technologies spread with amazing speed through Europe – as fast as, or faster than, the spread of technologies today.

Gutenberg had invented movable-type printing shortly before 1440. Only some thirty years later, the printers of Rome, of whom there were now too many, complained of overproduction and begged the Pope for subsidies. There was overproduction, too, in the Netherlands and Germany. The Bible, including the Old Testament, could now be read by many. It became available in translation, with the consequence that Luther, and humanists like Erasmus and Francis Bacon, could be read by all. No longer was the reading of select parts of the Bible a remote *mysterium* mumbled in Latin by a priest in the echoing chancel of an awing church.

Commercial power had begun to shift from Italy and South Germany north to the Dutch and later the British, and would continue to do so. For all the gold and silver from the Americas, Spain was to decline precipitously. By the eighteenth century, a French ambassador was to report back that the land of the Spanish monarchy was completely depopulated; that it had neither industry nor good faith; no police and little justice; that the people were lazy and unlaborious; that there were neither roads nor canals nor navigable rivers, and few vehicles. 'In a word, one can say that this land is at least two centuries behind all others.' One must explain that Spain had a tax of 15 per cent on exports in addition to a sales tax of 15 to 20 per cent – a total impost of 32 to 38 per cent. These, the result of royal greed and short-sightedness, turned the terms of trade decidedly against her. Spain had pledged her future revenues five or ten times over. By the end of the first quarter of the seventeenth century the game was up. Spain's bankruptcy ruined Genoa and also put an end to the wealth of her great creditor, the house of Fugger. She had also ruined herself and was never to recover her greatness.

Meanwhile, in this sixteenth century, mercantilism still reigned – that strange, half-voluntary alliance of kings and merchants in defence of gold for the country and themselves. The world expanded. In the arts, it was the middle of the Renaissance – a Catholic phenomenon. In matters of the mind it was an age of Humanism. And Humanism was itself a harbinger of the Enlightenment – essentially a Protestant phenomenon. Inductive science was rising from the ashes of the alchemists and from an unquestioning acceptance of Aristotelian deductions – such as that all heavenly bodies are attached to spheres and are spun round by an unmoved mover. Superstition mingled with reason: it is said that Napier invented logarithms to help him calculate the Number of the Beast.

But the peasant still tilled the soil of his master, or was evicted from it to permit sheep to graze. His master, in turn, too hidebound by tradition to improve the management of his estates, borrowed on mortgage from merchants to sustain a degree of luxury which he could really not afford. His manor was 'bound fast in a skin of parchment, / The wax continued hard, the acres melting.' If the estate was taken in forfeit from the nobleman by the merchant, he would sell surplus assets, raise rents and make it pay; he would, in fact, use the same techniques as corporations use today when they have taken over other corporations.

But while the nobles began to have to yield in wealth to merchants, they did not yield in status – whether worldly or high ecclesiastical. For who would not rather, kneeling, receive a knightly accolade from kings than, standing, be rich from button-making? Royalty was more magnificent than ever. It was, in Hugh Trevor-Roper's words, the 'carefree magnificence of kings and courtiers, who do not need to count because they do not have to earn'.[8]

More so than before, it was not their morality, but the daily practices of merchants that determined the theories of trade. The general conjunction referred to earlier – the comparability of return on any form of capital, and the equivalence of money – this conjunction which made *rational* speculation possible, was drawing closer. But it had not yet arrived. To arrive fully, it was necessary for the middle class to become an economically determining class.

Actual events brought this about. But, as in all history, the warp of real events was knit with the woof of events of the mind. This important event of the mind was to be the Reformation of the sixteenth century, and the tangled skein of attitudes which issued from it. According to some, the Reformation decided happenings; according to others, it only coincided with them. This is what we must consider before we can agree that all the bricks of which capitalism is built had been laid and mortared.

Notes

1 Karl Marx, *Capital*, vol. II. ed. Kerr, 1909, p. 412.
2 R. H. Tawney, *Religion and the Rise of Capitalism*, John Murray, London, 1926/1944, p. 43.
3 Fernand Braudel, *The Mediterranean World in the Age of Phillip II*, Harper & Rowe, New York and London, 1972, vol. 2, pp. 521–2.
4 Benjamin Nelson *The Idea of Usury*, 2nd edn, University of Chicago Press, Chicago, 1969.
5 Henry Pirenne, *Economic and Social History of Medieval Europe*, trans. I. E. Clegg, Routledge & Kegan Paul Ltd, London, 1936, pp. 129–30.
6 Antoninus, *Summa moralis* III.3,4,vii., III.1.6,i., II.1.16,iii. See Bede Jarrett, *St. Antonino and Mediaeval Economics*, 1914, p. 192, p. 68, pp. 255–7.
7 Sidney Homer, *A History of Interest Rates*, Rutgers University Press, New Brunswick, NJ, 1963.
8 H. Trevor-Roper, *Religion, the Reformation and Social Change*, Secker & Warburg, London, 1984, p. 59.

11

Capitalism and Enterprise

The Transnationalism of Money

As we have seen, interest, overheads and money had become more acceptable to church and society as independently rational standards. Refined monetary instruments were brought into being. There are, for example, records from 1514 to 1516 of the use of the *contractus trinus*, or triple contract, when this type of contract had already been in use for some forty years. It was a package of three agreements: a contract of partnership, tied to an insurance policy for the principal sum, and an insurance contract against fluctuating returns on the principal. It was also known as the *contractus Germanicus*, or *deutscher Vertrag*. In the business world it was sufficient to mention the 'German Contract' without having to give further details because it was known to almost always pay a guaranteed 5 per cent. It was more complete than any arrangement available today from any *single* financial agency. It did not, however, guarantee against inflation.[1]

It was now necessary to perfect the internal mechanisms of the system. Money had to have two other properties to make it function universally. The first, already referred to, was its use to compare the return from one kind of investment with another. The other was to make it transnational and independent. Transnational, so that a debt, wherever incurred, could be paid from any one country to any other. Independent, so that debits and credits could be divorced from the goods or services that had given them their origin.

This is not to say that religious factors were no longer important. As we shall try to show, they were. But from now on, remarkably, their role was, if anything, to be an engine, not as hitherto a brake.

Meanwhile, merchants were no less astute then than they are today. In the first half of the fourteenth century, and again in the first half of the fifteenth, two shrewd Florentine writers on business advised on the proper management of exchange: never owe in a currency which is appreciating; money is dear before harvest time; dear just before soldiers are due to receive their pay; dear when galleys are about to leave Genoa or Venice with cargo. It is also dear at times of fairs when merchants buy grain and wool. Therefore secure exchange either well before or after these events.[2]

Bills of exchange became generally negotiable instruments in the whole of Europe in the sixteenth century. Until then it had been usual to transmit bearer bills and bonds with due formality before a notary. The 'or bearer' formula (which meant that *any* bearer could encash the bill of indebtedness) came into extensive use in Flemish Antwerp about 1560.

But it had been in common use in Italy much earlier. One may, therefore, wonder which merchants, Italian or Flemish, were able to visualize abstract values more clearly. To visualize that a bill which merchant A had drawn on merchant B had no necessary connection with the physical goods which A had supplied to B was an act of the imagination. Money, that abstraction from goods, had hereby achieved its reality as an independent asset. It ceased to matter for what you owed a debt, or to whom: once you signed, you owed – no matter in whose hands the paper found itself. It was, at any rate, one of the important discoveries made by capitalism.

Because the export of bullion and the carriage of money from one realm to another was forbidden in the mercantilist world of the sixteenth century, bills of exchange through Antwerp and Lyons had to substitute for gold in international trade. Governments could forbid the export of bullion, or they could prohibit exchange transactions, but they could hardly do both without bringing all trade to a standstill. One of the ironies of mercantilism, with its worship of gold, was that it forced alternative methods of trading upon merchants in which gold played no significant part.

In consequence, 'dry exchange' developed. This, in its definition by Elizabethan law, meant the 'deliver[y of] money in one realme to be payd in another realme, where the deliverer seeketh not to employ his money either upon wares or otherwise but only to exchange his said money home againe with lucre' (profit). In other words, international settlements in which money itself, not the goods, was the commodity traded.

The stand of the Church on this matter was ambivalent. In 1570, the papacy officially maintained her condemnation of dry exchange. But she also declared that the interest charged by the discounter of a bill of exchange was lawful. It was payment for labour and risk – provided that the instrument actually transferred money from place to place. The condition was in practice meaningless: it was simple enough, as Tawney explains, to meet it by drawing a bill on one side of the street and getting it accepted on the other side.[3]

In addition, there were futures trading, arbitrage dealings and other devices. Gresham, Queen Elizabeth's trusted advisor, even anticipated the method now employed by central government banks to dampen exchange rate fluctutions by the timely buying and selling of foreign currencies. The method was not adopted then and it works only passably now – the Bretton Woods agreement of 1946 on fixed rates of exchange having been abandoned in 1971, to the deep regret and frequent tears of international buyers and sellers.

Officially, the Church still maintained her prohibition on the taking of interest. Even capitalists were confused by the usury laws of those days. For example, in 1560, Marcus Fugger, a Catholic, a grand-nephew of the famous Jacob Fugger 'the Rich' of Augsburg, and now himself head of the firm, wrote to his father-confessor: 'It would be wholly good if you could arrange that money was lent to me also free of interest, because I owe about one and a half million Gulden for which I am obliged to pay five, eight, or even ten per cent interest. On the other hand, the King of Spain owes me one million and will not either pay me interest or return the principal sum. What ought I to do?' If a Fugger did not know, who could? In the event, the King of Spain never returned the money he owed, and the house of Fugger never recovered.

Capitalism, the Reformation and the Protestant Ethic

Of Luther (1483–1546), an intemperate man, less need be said than can be. The civil sword, he wrote, shall be red and bloody, and no one need think that the world can be ruled without blood. For present purposes, his insistence that Faith alone is what matters, not Faith *and* Good Works, suffices. Luther cannot have been aware of the many consequences of his abbreviation. If individual faith is arbiter, can there be another judge? Who are the sinners, who the saviour, and what is the shape of redemption? What kind of man would thrive on the single judgement of his own self-reliant faith with no confessor other than a silent God?

Luther deferred to princes, but he disliked the high capitalists of his time. For the Fugger family of Augsburg – king-makers, Catholics, rich, powerful, transnational and agents of the Pope – he felt the abiding enmity of a narrow God-serving monk for His self-serving surrogates on earth. With crudeness as evident in English as in German, he called the Fugger establishment a *Fukkerei*.

On usury, Luther was contradictory. On the one hand, he thought it wrong. On the other he said that it was highly necessary for interest to be regulated everywhere. But to abolish it entirely would not be right either, 'for it can be made just'. In *Table Talk*, written a few years before he died, he said that not gospel, but the commands of princes and the advantage of the state must govern the terms of loans. Was not, in any case, a tiny usury – *ein Wucherlein* – perhaps in order?

Calvin took a much more definite stand some decades later. Usury is not unlawful, he said, except in so far as it contravenes brotherly love. Let *each one* place himself before God's judgement, and act according to his conscience. As to how much interest was all right, and when, let the laws of equity decide, not discussion.[4]

The change of emphasis was greater than it seems. Now it is the duty of each one, unaided by priestly authority, to seek the judgement of God for himself alone. The rate of interest is to be governed by equity rather than Deuteronomy. And so, whatever role Luther and Calvin may have intended for the churches, the remaining future judge between the public interest and the selfish deeds of men would turn out to be – the state. In this change of emphasis – by far not the churches' wish – we may, perhaps, find the origins of the canonization of the state in the nineteenth century and its degraded exercise of brutal power in the twentieth.

It should not be thought that the Protestant clergy became forgiving. It continued to thunder against usury from the pulpit. Calvin himself dealt with 'usurie as the apothecarie doth with poison'.[5] Calvin, the stern disciplinarian, was no parent of laxity. But Calvin made a fresh start: the Mosaic law may have suited the Jews but it was no longer relevant to daily commerce. The difference was that he sanctioned interest – provided the borrower gained as much advantage from the loan as the lender.

What did 'as much' mean and how much was 'much'? The floodgates were opened; who now could nicely judge the balance of advantage in other than extreme cases? The middle classes obtained a spiritual charter for the bourgeois revolution. True, the charter was conditional because, having overthrown monasticism, Calvinism's aim was to 'turn the secular world into a gigantic monastery',[6] a divinely inspired police state. In it, few unprescribed activities and enjoyments were to be allowed. In one town, Geneva, 150 persons were burned at the stake in sixty years, including a child for striking its parents.[7] But the permissive nod had been noted – nod conditional or nod unconditional.

Business success was thought to be a blessing. A blessing not for joy but for duty; not for oneself but as trustee for God – with only local temporary possession until He would descend to claim his own. All prayed for this. Indeed and amen, but it was not taken to be a serious business risk.

And so business sailed with a full spread of canvas before the new wind toward the future – without, then as now, a fathom line of settled values.

Henceforward the Protestant church was often to become an ecclesiastical arm of the state, heeded but no longer unquestioned. It still attempted to dispose of men's conduct, but it became on occasions almost trivial, as when, in the 1680s, it tried to rule on the 'weighty problem whether boys of sixteen might wear their hats in church, and by what marks one might detect a witch'.[8]

In the end, it was not Calvinism's habit of austerity that bent history to a new course. It was, instead, the habit of gainful work and the application of a remorseless logic to its fruits. This is what the doctrine had taught Swiss Calvinists, French Huguenots, and English and Scottish Puritans. Above all, this is what it had taught the austere New England Puritans who condemned unfair trade with all except the Children of the Devil. Native North American Indians, scalped of all but the skins of their skulls, were of course classified as this particular variety of Satan's seed. And throughout – then and for the next four hundred years – almost every variety of belief exempted the whipped and fettered bodies of African slaves from the blessings of its righteousness.

Meanwhile, Catholics also bent with the winds of change. Counter-Reformation Jesuits, if not with hearts then with eyes wide open to events, relaxed the rules against the modes of commerce – not to encourage the capitalist spirit but because they were realists.

Capitalism had, after all, flourished even before the Reformation in Flemish Antwerp and in neighbouring Liège; in Portuguese Lisbon; in South German Augsburg; in Milan and other towns of Italy. Capitalism was not an invention of the Protestant mind alone. Credit for its achievements was not to be surrendered lightly to the new apostates.

What concerns us now is not the logic of capitalism, but its acceptance. Tawney says that Calvin's doctrine 'took with the brethren like polygamy with the Turks'. It spread to England, whose Calvinist connection began shortly before the exile in Switzerland of English Protestants during the five-year reign of Catholic Queen Mary ('Bloody Mary') from 1543 to 1548. One Swiss authority shows that this exile was the university of English theologians. Many of those who were to occupy leading offices under Mary's Anglican successor, Elizabeth I, had sat at the feet of the Swiss Fathers, certainly at Calvin's and at Bullinger's.[9] They included eight who were to become English bishops and archbishops, one who became Queen Elizabeth's private chaplain, and one who was to be a senior ambassador.

The Coming of Free Enterprise

By the middle of the sixteenth century there had been enough rehearsal of the rationale of money. Add to this that Jews, though their faith, too, had many legends in it, set most of them aside in daily work and did not mythify reality. Sombart said that capitalism *was* Judaism. He was in error; as Paul Johnson points out, the Middle Ages were not to end for the Jews until the last decades of the eighteenth century.

But the thesis that Calvinism and Puritanism of themselves led to a flowering of business everywhere cannot be sustained. Where the churches kept their grip, as they did in Scotland, progress was halted. What mattered more than Catholic or Protestant doctrine was freedom of conscience in places where there was also freedom of action. Business flourished in towns and countries where these coincided. Francis Bacon asked whether 'the tooth of usury be grinded, that it bite not too much', and answered that this would do about as much practical good as that usurers should wear orange-tawny bonnets.[10]

Significantly, the practice of private confession of sins was declared by Calvin no longer a sacrament. This meant that sin became the personal on-board baggage of each traveller to the end of life's journey. Furthermore, Calvinism believed in predestination, ineluctable predestination: if you were not one of the Elect, you were born to be damned – damned for ever without any chance of redemption. The only outward sign of Grace was success.

Think of what this means: there is no longer an escape from your preordained fate. You may be one of the damned if you do, or one of the damned if you don't; equally, you may be one of the blessed if you do, or one of the blessed if you don't. If you are a sharp-dealing businessman, there is no man, no priest, no confessor, with whom to share your consciousness of sin, from whom to seek forgiveness. It is proper to be self-righteous because you yourself are the only confidant and judge you have. 'Lack of self-confidence is the result of insufficient faith, hence of imperfect grace.'[11] You worship God because he is powerful and to do him honour but not because he is loving and forgiving. The god of the Elect had again become the jealous tribal god of the Old Testament. All this was not the official doctrine of any church. But to throw Calvin's legacy into high relief is not to falsify it.[12]

We recognize this breed of man as one who lives and breathes today. This breed that denies itself the enjoyments of private life for the sake of achievement in business; this breed of 'inward ascetics', with *innerweltlicher Askese*, as Max Weber called it; this asceticism that scores the measure of its self-denial by the growth of profits. At its best, of course, such renouncement breeds fair and conscientious business leaders. At its worst, it breeds tyrants who, in Evelyn Underhill's words, follow an 'unknown God whom [they] so coldly serve'.

Had the Church not made a business of salvation, the Reformation might not have occurred. In such an event (though the matter is not capable of proof) would the flowering of capitalism have been nipped? A form of it is likely to have emerged in any case: was the sale of indulgences by professional pardoners not itself evidence of business-mindedness?

But, as said, the thesis that Calvinism and Puritanism of themselves lead to a flowering of business everywhere cannot be sustained. Even Max Weber, who wrote so persuasively about the Protestant Ethic, said that he would not maintain 'such a foolish and doctrinaire thesis' as that the spirit of capitalism could only have arisen as a result of the Reformation, or even that capitalism as an economic system was an effect of the Reformation.[13]

We must in passing note a curious point. A man who believes in complete predestination – that everything in this world is foreordained – must act exactly as though he completely believed in 'free will' without predestination. He does not know *what* is foreordained. And so, even though he believes that *whatever* happens is bound to happen, he is still bound to choose the 'whatever' that is 'bound' to happen. In practice, therefore, this gives the predestinationist Puritan and Calvinist businessman great moral freedom and flexibility. The paradox of preordination is illustrated by Thomas More's story about the good citizen of Almayn (Germany) who had robbed a man. He admitted his crime before the court but pleaded that it had been his destiny to commit it. Therefore they should not blame him. The court answered that, just as it was his destiny to steal, so it was the court's destiny to hang him for it.

Yet the connection between religion and the growth of capitalism cannot be completely discounted. The connection was, perhaps, indirect. The new creed created new men: Huguenots, Calvinists, Puritans, other Nonconformists. It created new social attitudes, a new social type, and, of course, a new and numerous class. They were not always men of inward asceticism, as Weber thought, because some good Calvinists lived exceedingly well. But many of them were alienated from the rest of the populace by their religious differences, even when at home.

In the event, many of them had to leave home, or were forced to flee abroad. They were uprooted or displaced, emigrants or immigrants. But, having business training and experience, they were at home in commerce even if not at home in where they lived. They were able to look at the world without the baggage of patriotism, native legend or inward constraint. They were able to look cooly at their new home with the pure rationale of how to make their money work profitably.

To follow the details of these diasporas would take us far beyond our short review. There were the Huguenots who fled to Switzerland from France; Jews from Portugal and Spain to the north; Flemings from Liège to the Baltic and to Hamburg; South Germans from Augsburg to France; dissenting Italians who fled from Milan and

Lucca to Switzerland; some Catholics, some Jews, but mostly Protestants – uncomfortable dissenters, dispersed, banished, dismissed and often killed. The historian Hugh Trevor-Roper[14] argues that the old economic elite of Europe was driven into heresy because the attitude of mind which it had harboured for generations, and which had been tolerated for generations – the humanist spirit of Erasmus (1466–1536) – 'was suddenly, in some places, declared heretical and intolerable'. This attitude suffused the beliefs of this elite, but did not inhibit it from the pursuit and attainment of success in its new land. Erasmus, they say, laid the eggs; Luther and his heirs raised the chickens.

Even today, people whose actual or inherited roots are elsewhere – the Chinese of Indonesia and Malaysia, Europeans in America in the late nineteenth and early twentieth centuries, the Irish in American politics, the Armenians, Chinese and Vietnamese in America today, expatriate Hungarians in the sciences and in economics almost everywhere, *pieds noirs* or Algeria-born Frenchmen in metropolitan France, as also Albert Einstein, Karl Marx, Joseph Conrad and Vladimir Nabokov – displayed and still display the talents of the *emigré*. If we add previous centuries, more can be found: almost all immigrant Americans, Baltic Germans in Russia, Swedes in Finland – not to mention the ancient Greeks in Roman banking.

Universalism vanished in the seventeenth century. The universalism of the Church and the internationalism of late medieval and Renaissance commerce ceased. It was from now on replaced by the particular and separate interests of national states. With little proof, State and Church alike had maintained for centuries that the taking of interest was wrong, now, with equal lack of proof, that it was right.

It was an unquiet century, a century of wars. Financial markets were perfected by the need for money to pursue them. The Bank of England, for example, started from a need to raise money to fight the French: a duty was to be raised on shipping tonnage as security for any lenders of one-and-a-fifth million pounds to the government. The lenders were given another privilege: a charter of incorporation as Governor & Company of the Bank of England. The charter was to lapse when the loan had been repaid. The loan was never repaid and the bank survived.

By now, making money was the fulfilment of man's calling. Men were told (by Baxter's *Christian Directory* in 1678, for example) that if

God showed them a way in which they could lawfully make more, and they chose a less gainful way, they crossed one of the ends of their calling and thereby refused to be 'God's steward'. About a century later, the father of Methodism, John Wesley, repeated the message: 'We must exhort all Christians to gain all they can, and save all they can; that is, to grow rich.'

These calls to maximize the return on funds employed is precisely what any school of business administration teaches today. It may do so without reference to the same High Authority, of course, but with almost the same degree of sanctification. We have arrived at modern capitalism.

The web of events is tangled and causes, as we have seen, are rarely in the singular. When we mix the leaven of causes with the lump of history, we find that our escape from the confinement of old guilts and old ideas was very slow. No single event altered history's course without a ripeness of the times and many gathered prior tensions.

It is dangerously innocent to believe otherwise, because the devil is not one but many. Attempts to reduce history to just one devil, just one culprit, or just a few conspirators, has only led to the burning of witches in the sixteenth and seventeenth centuries, and the gassing of Jews in the twentieth.

Notes

1. H. M. Robertson, *The Rise of Economic Individualism*, Cambridge University Press, Cambridge, 1933.
2. Pegollotti, *Practica della mercature* 1335–43, and Uzzaro, also *Practica della mercature* 1442.
3. Thomas Wilson, *Discourse on Usury*, 1572, introduction by R. H. Tawney, Cass & Co., London, 1925, p. 136.
4. ibid., p. 118.
5. R. H. Tawney, *Religion and the Rise of Capitalism*, John Murray, London, 1926/1944, p. 106.
6. ibid., p. 115.
7. Paul Henry, *Das Leben des Johannes Calvins*, 1838, pp. 70–5.
8. Tawney, *Religion and the Rise of Capitalism*, p. 217.
9. J. C. Moerikofer, *Geschichte der evangelischen Fluechtlinge in der Schweiz*, Leipzig, 1876.
10. Francis Bacon, *Essays*, XLI.
11. Max Weber, *The Protestant Ethic and the Spirit of Capitalism* (1904–5), ed. Talcott Parsons, 1930, ch. IV.

12 See, for example, the 'Westminster Confession' of 1647, ch. III.3. 'By the decree of God . . . some men and angels are predestined unto everlasting life, and others foreordained to everlasting death.'
13 Weber, *The Protestant Ethic*, ch. III.
14 Hugh Trevor-Roper, *Religion, the Reformation, and Social Change*, Secker & Warburg, London, 1984, p. 27. Closely argued and persuasive. See pages 1–46.

Section 5
Cultures that Shaped Business

Preamble

Differences rather than similarities place the Jews and the Japanese in adjacent chapters. Japanese civilization, indigenous and vigorous, is well fitted for great enterprises and orderly array. Not so Jewish civilization through the ages before the nineteenth century: how, asked Max Weber in his *Sociology of Religion*, does one explain the fact that no pious Jew succeeded before the nineteenth century in establishing a large industry employing Jewish workers of the ghettos at times when numerous Jewish 'proletarians' were present there, when princely patents and privileges could be bought for the establishment of any sort of industry and when areas of industrial activity uncontrolled by guild monopoly were open?

The entrepreneur, Sombart maintained, is conqueror, organizer and trader – three in one. Their circumstances in the lands of strangers speciated and kept the Jews in trade, beyond which they could not achieve much but within which they could, at times at least, preserve their identity and beliefs. By contrast, since the Meiji Restoration in 1868, and especially after the Second World War, Japanese civilization – coherent, organic and domestic – could capture all three Sombartian attributes of entrepreneurship. The Japanese, unlike the Jews, could harness individual abilities in the service of all, and did not have to suffer the thwarting of their ablest minds by discontinuities, separateness and alienation.

To understand today's Japanese, we look at their past, and more at their pleasures than their history. Why is the short-lived blossom of the cherry tree revered? Because beauty, as Donald Keene points out, is irregular, simple and perishable. It prefers to suggest rather than define.[1] Beauty suggests: only beginnings and ends are interesting;

ripeness and completeness is boring. It is irregular: symmetry deadens. It is simple: less is more, natural timber lovingly joined is rarer and more costly than gold leaf and cupids. It is perishable: beauty is small and fleeting.

The contrast between this ideal and the reality of industrial, corporate, concrete-clad Japan is great. Japanese pursuit of comfort, status, security and money is more in evidence than aesthetics. Modern Japanese, like Westerners, want their luxuries. The difference is that, historically, luxury in the West was elaborate, in Japan simple. Compared with rising incomes, Western luxuries are becoming less expensive in Japan. But the cost of Japanese luxury is now too high for any but a favoured few.

This section's theme is Japan's change, industrial and partly social, from easternness to westering.

Note

1 Donald Keene, *The Pleasures of Japanese Literature*, Columbia University Press, New York and Guildford, Surrey, 1988, ch. 1.

12

The Jews: A Dispersed Culture

The Business Outsiders

Some writers, like Sombart, have given the role of the Jews in history a headline; others, a mere footnote.

The history of the Jews is not itself economic history, despite their role in it. It is in part the history of a very persevering and persistent theology, and it is in part a history of many curtailed migrations; in part, also, it is a history of individual and collective economic disasters. The stage was not theirs, nor the play, but they acted their part with a fastidiousness peculiar to themselves. Whereas the capitalism of Catholic bankers and Nonconformist Protestants was a capitalism of the structure, their capitalism was a capitalism of the gaps.

It is also the history of a people that has spent the greater part of its existence in dispersion among other nations – Egypt, Babylon, Rome, Alexandria, Babylon (Persia) again, Europe. This scattering, writes Joseph Klausner, occurred not only because the kings of Assyria and Babylon uprooted some Israelites and Judeans from their land, but also 'because of a voluntary dispersion for the purpose of business and financial gain'.[1] He quotes the Jewish philosopher and historian Philo (born about 5–10 BC) to the effect that Jerusalem had many 'colonies' in Egypt, Phoenicia, Syria, more distant Pamphylia, Cilicia and Asia Minor as far as Bithynia. In the same manner in Europe, Thessaly, Boeotia, Macedonia, Attica, Corinth and 'all the most fertile and wealthiest districts of Peloponnesus'; celebrated islands such as Cyprus and Crete; countries beyond the Euphrates; Babylon 'and all the satrapies around, which have any advantage whatever of soil or climate'. Their very dispersion constituted a commercial information system with many correspondents.

From the second century and for several centuries thereafter, when Jewish resistance to the Romans had finally been broken, they may even be considered to have lived as exiles in their own country, Palestine. Paul Johnson[2] reports that at the time of Caligula (37–41 AD) hellenized, anti-Jewish Gentiles were the elite of Palestine, and that they, rather than the Jews, supplied the rich men, the merchants, the local civil service and tax collectors. From the middle of the third century, quiet acceptance of Gentile government became official Jewish doctrine. In the course of the millenia, exilic life must have become as much a norm as an exception for them. On this larger scale, however, their own economic history became part of the economic history of the nations amongst whom they lived.

A minor gloss may be made at this point. Deuteronomy (23:20) declares that a Jew may lend to a stranger at interest, but no interest is to be taken from a co-religionist brother. Less celebrated, but equally pertinent, are two other passages in Deuteronomy (15:1–3; 15:6), which seem to command that at the end of every seven years he shall release all his debtors from their debts to him. Every creditor who lends anything to his neighbour shall release the debt; he shall not exact it of his neighbour, or of his brother; but he may exact it again of a foreigner. Deuteronomy also permits him to lend to many nations but not to borrow.

Taken together, these are very unattractive commercial conditions. Domestically, you may not earn interest on your loans. Even then, these loans are to be completely written off every seventh year. Having had to write them off, you are not yourself to borrow, even if a 'brother' is prepared to lend you money. But then, considering the terms, why would he?

On the other hand, dealing with 'strangers' is liberalized: lending money at interest is approved and there is no need to write off money lent. These are powerful incentives to take business out of the native land and live where business does not breach holy laws. The remark is irreverent, but, given that a Jewish merchant of the time was a literal and pious man, his conclusion may easily have been that Rome or Alexandria was a preferable business address with fewer disincentives.

The Jews, from antiquity to modern times, breathed the spirit of their holy Book as much as they breathed the air of their country of sojourn. The Jews in exile were a nomocracy, a people governed by a code and by sacred hopes. The land of their Messiah and the landscape of Zion was a vision – an ideal landscape of the imagination, against which any real landscape paled into mere territoriality.

Now, before it sees an ideal landscape, imagination asks what landscape, what Eden, it *should* be seeing. It is, in other words, concerned with values before it is concerned with things. It predisposes thought to an inward arrangement of reality. It encourages an ability of the mind to combine and recombine – an ability which is one of the marks of the entrepreneurial mind. With this ability, one might have supposed that the Jews would achieve much in business. Unfortunately for them, the inward and outward obstacles of subsequent history were too great and too debilitating. 'They often saw the world outside with clearer eyes than it saw itself; but when the Jews turned inward, on themselves, their eyes misted over, their vision became opaque.'[3] There were periods – as in the sixteenth century – when they lapsed into irrationality and 'a glutinous mass of magic-mystic lore'. Their achievements in business, before their emancipation, were wide but marginal.

Their long endurance of inferior status, in the expectation that a messiah would one day come to establish them in honour, is an example of present generations accepting suffering for the benefit of coming generations.

Usury, Persecution and Competition

Perhaps, for all their tribulations, the Jews persisted as traders for the very reason that land, and the exaltation of aristocracy, were denied them. Except from the late nineteenth century – a time when aristocracy began to turn into the empty symbol which it is today – they could never aspire to high status. In this, they were not unlike German merchants of the Baroque and after, who also had to abandon any thought of preferment because the Prussian landed nobility would not have merchants at any price. They had, therefore, generation after generation, to stick to their business and their bourgeois status. German merchants and manufacturers accepted this constraint and did well, unlike British and French merchants whose enterprise was thinned, in the second or third generation, by ascent to 'higher', uncommercial ranks.

According to Sombart, 'Judaism never formulated a poverty ideal.'[4]

They had their own proletariat but they were socially too cohesive to admit to it. Their religion demanded self-respect; the Sabbath-eve meal was to be decorously middle class, even though the Jewish pedlar or porter and his family might have to skimp for the rest of the week. On the other hand, once the constraints had been removed, this *embourgeoisement*, this middle-classness, gave them an immediate common denominator with their non-Jewish middle-class business neighbours. When the time came, it did not make them better liked, but it made them better understood.

In the Middle Ages and for many years thereafter the Jews were regarded with displeasure because they seemed to have cash when all others only had some land – except the Church, which had both land and money. Until at least the eighteenth century, Jews were the retail bankers to the poor. They were resented by the mass of common men because they were lenders close to the common man – while Christian bankers dealt with kings. Having to borrow as a result of some natural disaster – drought, flood, plague – was in itself a disaster. The little people, when their crops failed and when they desperately needed money to survive saw the moneylending, pawn-broking Jew, and they remembered the high usurious interest of this lender of last and only resort.

Expulsions were frequent. They were, for example, banished from England in 1290 – all 16,511 of them – because, in the words of an old historian, 'they were generally disagreeable to the people.' But even then, as the following contemporary incident demonstrates, English law permitted no inhumanity beyond banishment. It is best told by a Dr Tovey, in words he wrote in 1738:

Upon banishment, the richest of the Jews embarked themselves, with their treasure, in a tall ship of great Burthen; when it was under sail, and gotten down the Thames, towards the mouth of the river, beyond Queenborough, the Master of it, confederating with some of the mariners, invented a strategem to destroy them. And to bring the same to pass, commanded to cast anchor, and rode at the same, till the ship, at low water, lay upon the sands: and then pretending to walk on shore for his health and diversion, invited the Jews to go along with him; which they, nothing suspecting, readily consented to; and continued there till the tide began to come in again; which as soon as the Master perceived, he privily stole away, and was again drawn up into the ship, as had been before concerted. But the Jews, not knowing the danger, continued to amuse themselves as before. Till at length, observing how fast the tide came in upon them, they crowded all to the ship's side, and called out for help. When he, like a profane villain, instead of giving them assistance, scoffingly made answer that they ought rather to call upon Moses, by whose conduct their fathers passed through the Red Sea, and who was still able to deliver them out of those raging floods which came in upon them: and so, without saying more, leaving them to the mercy of the waves, they all miserably perished. But the fact coming, some how or other, to be known, the miscreants were afterwards tryed for it, by the Justices Itinerant in Kent, convicted of murder and hanged.[5]

Four hundred years later the Jews were permitted to return to England.

The Jews were actors with peculiar and particular parts, but not actors in their own plays. Had the Jews not existed, it is at least possible that other actors would have mounted the stage of economic history to fill their roles, even though these roles were without honour until approximately the Austrian Edict of Toleration of 1781, and until the rise to eminence of such bankers as the Rothschilds in the nineteenth century, when one of the French branch of the family, in 1905, even became banker to the Holy See in Rome.

This displacement by other actors constantly happened when the game became profitable enough. According to Henry Pirenne,[6] for example, the pawnbroking Jews of the thirteenth century encountered powerful competition from Frenchmen – the men of Cahors – and from the Italians of Lombardy. The Cahorsins became so infamous in the France of those days that 'cahorsins' became the synonym for moneylenders. The Lombards of Italy (originally the Langobardians, a 'barbaric' Germanic tribe that invaded Italy in the second half of the sixth century) had, in the course of the centuries, learnt to be quite unbarbarically talented in money matters. A little of their imprint remains: the city of London had its 'Lombard' loans, and still has its Lombard Street. The Germans today still speak of a 'Lombard rate' – an interest rate some fifty points higher than the central bank's discount rate.

In return for a rent, says Pirenne, princes and towns granted the Lombards the right to set up 'loan tables', benches, *banco*, bank. The earliest of these grants in the Low Countries goes back to 1280. The Lombards thereby gained a monopoly which excluded others, such as '*toscans, cavorsins, juis*'. One may infer that it was often their persuasions which contributed to bring about the expulsion of the Jews, whose place they took. Although the earliest grants required that loans should be made 'well and loyally without malice or usury', in practice it meant loans in conformity with 'the usages and customs according to which the Lombards are accustomed to lend'.[7] That rate was 43.5 per cent per annum – almost double the rate of commercial interest. The Jews moved on.

Notes

1. Joseph Klausner, *From Jesus to Paul*, Allen & Unwin, London, 1944, p. 8.
2. Paul Johnson, *A History of the Jews*, Weidenfeld & Nicholson, London, 1987, p. 136.
3. ibid., p. 287.
4. W. Sombart (Der Bourgeois), *The Quintessence of Capitalism*, trans. M. Epstein, London, 1915.
5. Quoted by Sir Alfred Denning in *Freedom under the Law*, Stevens & Sons Ltd, London, 1949, from *Anglia Judaica*, 1738.
6. Henry Pirenne, *Economic and Social History of Medieval Europe*, trans. I. E. Clegg, Routledge & Kegan Paul Ltd, London, 1936, pp. 133–6.
7. G. Bigwood, *Le Commerce de l'argent*, Brussels, 1921–2, vol. 1, p. 340.

13

The Japanese: A Clustered Culture

A Sun Lately Risen

'Are they with Force unable to invade? No matter; they'll undo the world by Trade,' went an English ballad of 1667 on the wealth of the Dutch. As already said, the Dutch of the seventeenth century, though they lived on a small piece of territory with few natural resources, were yet able to outdo the English in trade – with the Baltic, the Middle East, and with India and China. The Dutch sold well because they bought well; they were trained and educated and had an infrastructure second to none. And they were engrossed in trade – merchants, craftsmen, government. There were no distractions and no aristocratic aspirations. They applied themselves. One can hardly look for identity in comparing a small country in the seventeenth century with Japan in the twentieth, but it will serve as analogue.

Japan is new to us; the Western experience of her as an economic force is only a quarter of a century old – the years since she began to affect us massively. Thirty years or so ago she was a remote curiosity.

The landscapes of history through which she passed in her long voyage from feudalism to intensive industrialization were so varied, so diverse, that Japan is, in many respects, almost as new to the Japanese as she is to us.

Feudalism of various degrees lasted in Japan, but died elsewhere. Had feudalism continued in Europe for as long as in Japan, instead of ceasing some 350 years earlier, Western industrialism, individualistic and renitent, might have taken other forms, though it is idle to speculate whether Western and Japanese institutions might therefore have converged.

The peace of the second half of this century imposed on Japan's rulers the high civility which had always been the hallmark of her common man. We see Japan today as a country paternalistically resolute in her pursuit of economic achievement and tranquillity for her people. But it would be wrong to believe that this concern for her people is an historic habit.

For at least the last one thousand years, Japanese government passed from an uncaring aristocratic regime, through feudal rule and frequent internecine wars, to the Meiji Restoration of 1868. Before the restoration her common people suffered great abuse. And since then, also, they for many years endured most of the excesses of industrialization that had befallen Britain decades earlier.

The condition of the common man in the Heian era, which started about a thousand years ago, was dire. His life, so Ivan Morris tells us, was close to the Hobbesian state of nature – an existence 'nasty, poore, brutish and short'. He was illiterate, ridden by fears and superstitions, ignorant of anything beyond his narrow experience. His day was spent in unremitting work on the land without profit to himself and his family. His monotony was relieved only by marriages, births, deaths and Shinto festivals. 'The riches of Chinese culture, the profound teachings of Buddhism, and the civilized amenities of the capital might as well have belonged to a different planet for all the effects they had on his rough, cheerless life. During the few hours spent away from the fields he and his kind were as a rule crowded together in dark, noisome hovels, where they ate and slept on bare boards.'[1] His food was of the coarsest; those who commanded him were not inclined to let him enjoy the fruits of his labour, and history reports many sumptuary edicts of the type: 'Farmers [are] forbidden to eat fish or drink wine.'

The Heian empire was an age of an extreme refinement of manners for the aristocracy. It was an age whose cult was 'an awareness of beauty so sharp that it was poignant'. But it was a sense of beauty devoid of any sense of charity, and its delicacy of taste was sapped of energy. The 'heart of things' was the sadness of beauty (*mono no aware*) – roughly what Virgil meant by *lacrimae rerum*, 'the sense of tears in mortal things'. Sometimes, even today, this sense of dainty arrest in art, of slender aestheticism, still fleetingly touches our perception of Japan.

The neglect of the common man continued in the subsequent feudal centuries. Any complaint was dealt with brutally. In 1651, Sakura Sogoro, a poor farmer, presented a petition to the Shogun himself on behalf of 300 of his fellows oppressed by their lord. The guilty baron was punished for his misrule, but Sogoro and his wife were crucified, after first seeing his children beheaded.[2]

The Industrial Revolution in Japan

Lafcadio Hearn was an extraordinary Greek with an Irish education who made a career in American journalism. He went to Japan, married a Japanese and became a Japanese citizen. In later life he also became a distinguished scholar and sympathetic observer of Japanese life. He was one of that small band of foreigners, mainly Americans, who fashioned the mould in which contemporary Japan was later cast.

In 1904, he observed that instead of the ancient kindly relations between master and workers, all the horrors of factory life at its worst had been brought into existence – with no legislation to restrain inhumanity. The new combinations of capital had re-established servitude under harsher forms than ever were imagined under the feudal era. The misery of the women and children subjected to that servitude was a public scandal, and 'proved strange possibilities of cruelty on the part of people once renowned for their kindness'.[3]

Eleven years later things had not improved. Another observer, Baroness Shidzue Ishimoto, described the darkness, the heat and moisture that reigned in the subterranean world of mines. The roof of the pit dropped to less than four feet. Naked men sat on their knees digging coal with their picks. Wives and daughters of miners went down half-naked, mingling with the naked men labourers. They followed the men and carried the coal as the men loosened it with their picks. Women who worked in the darkness had a 'pale complexion like the skin of a silkworm'. They were shameless, the last sign of feminine dignity sloughing off. Often, pregnant women, working until the last moment, gave birth to children in the dark pit.

It would be hard, continued this observer, to tell the difference between the life of pigs and the life of these miners. One barrack was usually divided into booths to house from five to seven families. Each one of these booths was about 12 feet square, separated from the adjoining booth by thin boards. The average size of one family was five or six members, and there was only one lavatory for a whole row of barracks. There was neither gas nor water, and the summer heat of South Japan was unbearable in such conditions.

The people who lived in these barns were strictly watched and loyalty to their employers was enforced. It was impossible for them to run away. The miners were usually desperate. They saw no hope for the future. Men and their wives quarrelled a great deal. Men beat women and children. Many men drank all their pay. 'Who dare preach family obligations to men who got only $20 for a month's work?' And that was eight dollars more than the maximum allowed to women.

Such was Shidzue Ishimoto's description of conditions at the Mitsui coal mines at Miike in Southern Japan between 1915 and 1917. Her husband, the son of a samurai general of the Imperial Army had – with the self-sacrificial idealism of some upper-class Japanese of his day – chosen to be a mining engineer at an initial net salary of $21.50 per month.[4]

Compare her description with another, by Miriam Beard,[5] of children who were left in the hands of brutal overseers, to be underfed on rancid bacon, worked as many as eighteen hours a day, put in irons or whipped, kept prisoners. It is a description of ignorant, stunted infants, who stood whimpering at their machines from dawn until deep at night, with scarcely a pause to eat. 'Their one friend, death, was a constant visitor to the mills.' In the mines, too, children toiled along with half-naked men and women, pushing up steep and slimy tunnels the heavy coal-cars, the weight of which made sores on their tender foreheads. They seldom saw the light of the sun. If they survived to become adults, their lot was hardly improved.

Although this last description is not of Japan but of England in the age of the early Industrial Revolution, it is as searing, as pitiable – and indistinguishable.

Lafcadio Hearn had concluded that 'the future Japan must rely upon the least amiable qualities of her character for success in the universal struggle.' Has she, is the question.

The impression of this practical businessman is that Japan's main continuity has been a continuity of isolation. It is his impression, also, that of all the developed countries of the world, Japan's present socio-industrial and socio-political structure is one of the least ancient. Most of what is important to Japan today is new, not old, and the most important is the improved condition of her millions.

That is not to say that her history is irrelevant: revolutions happen when a surfeit of distress is moved to action by new alternatives. These questions lead to the mind of Japan.

The Mind of Japan

In 1961, the year of the writer's first acquaintance with Japan, Tokyo taxis, all classes of them, were boxy, self-powered *rikishas*, driven with unavailing fury against all other taxi-enemies. This was in itself a change from older days, a mere forty years before, when no young fleet-footed rickshaw man, with delicate respect for age, would overtake an older, slower colleague.

Japan's voice is clear in little things; in the meaning of the tea ceremony, perhaps, which, by a 'brief revelation of almost perfect peace', makes life a work of art. The tea ceremony, so Kakuzo reminds us in the *Book of Tea*, is the adoration of the imperfect, a tender attempt to accomplish something possible in this impossible thing known as life. 'In the liquid amber within the ivory-porcelain' men can feel the littleness of great things in themselves and, by this means, the greatness of little things in others.

There is a sense of the fleetingness of things in Japan. Japanese woodcuts, a form of non-aristocratic art intended for the middle classes, were called *Ukiyo-E*, pictures from a floating world. The woodcut began to appear in the eighteenth century for the entertainment of those who found classical art too severe. Themselves confined, the middle classes wanted windows on the world around them. They wanted gossip and a little titillation. With the woodcut, the Japanese may claim to have been the inventors of comics and strip cartoons. Still, though they were enjoyed, they were pictures of shifting and ephemeral events which, alongside the solemnity of daily life, did not amount to more than evanescent footprints in the sands of time.

The Japanese are not intellectually passionate. They distrust the artificial coherence of philosophical, religious or political dogmas and they do not believe that even the most persuasive definition of the eternal describe the nature of eternity. They admit that there is truth, more properly, that there are truths, but truths in their own time and their own place, and not the same truths in all imaginable circumstances. Nothing should be taken to extremes – not even an ideal – since there is no knowable perfection but only temporary excellence. To Karl Marx, with his certainty about the direction of the march of history, Japan would have been a disappointment.

Individually, the Japanese are one of the world's most honest people. Japanese national government is not: the pork barrel is tapped to pay for the good graces of electorates. And as to Japanese business, the plainest answer to the question whether it is honest is yes. But the answer is not always plain; it is a yes which depends on definitions. When the Japanese serve their master, their personal honesty is overlaid by their duty to him. No is then not no but the absence of yes. Yes itself, if not defined on paper, is yes according to the rules of Japanese life and business practice. Honesty does not become itself an absolute. But on money owed, Japanese business is more scrupulous than any. If one has picked right and understood the deal, business with Japan is pleasurable.

Put more bluntly: when Japanese agree they do not agree in quite the Western sense. They agree in the sense that the general consensus agrees. The same applies to truth; truth is what is valid for the purpose, what fits the times, what fits life. Therefore, if the logic of the situation alters, if a new paradigm emerges (as happened after the Second World War and may be happening now); if, in short, the ideal changes, so will the truth which appertains to it. Western businessmen are sometimes puzzled by what they feel are unexpected changes after long cooperation. It is their own fault for not having a fine enough feel for tides which to the Japanese are obvious. To the Japanese, it is as though nature herself is pragmatic and not, as in the Western view, constant and eternal. The Japanese take an ironic view of ultimate ends, but they take a very serious view of the means to achieve them.

Their pragmatism is, in an incongruous sense, spiritualized. The Japanese way has its parallels in Calvinism, or, at least, with Calvinism as interpreted by important historians and sociologists.[6] Calvinism, so goes the argument, was not opposed to the accumulation of wealth, or to the charging of interest within the limits of decency and charity, provided one worked. Work had spiritual value, and wealth was a proof of effort and God's Grace. But there was to be frugality: the profits from work were to be devoted to investment and further growth, but not to luxury or conspicuity. Work was not for joy; work was a constant duty and a proof of faith. While the Roman Catholic merchant often regarded wealth as a proof of power, the respectable Calvinistic Puritan saw it as proof of decent standing. All this was not very different from the Japanese concept of life in duty, provided we remember that the Protestant ethic in the West applied to individuals, but in Japan applies to aggregations.

It is said that religion consists in believing that *everything* that happens is extraordinarily important. This is true of the Japanese attitude to work. Duty comes before all; first to the family; next to the village, which has today become the company in which they serve. Not least, there is a duty to oneself – the '*giri* to one's name': a definite *noblesse oblige* to keep one's honour bright within one's station. This sensitivity, including sensitivity to slights, is oddly unique to Japan. The Chinese and other Asian peoples, when they take offence, react robustly and do not brood. But in Japan one must not shame a man. Good-humoured banter is the limit. Sarcastic, sardonic, cynical speech is not recommended for strangers in Japan.

Or, for that matter, shouting: in Japan, the one who shouts his argument is said to have lost his case already. And it is best not to read only pleasure into a smile. A smile can, and mostly does, betoken pleasure, as elsewhere. There is more smiling in Japan than in most other countries. But equally it can betoken pain, as nowhere else, except perhaps in Indonesia. 'The Japanese smile at first charms. It is only at a later day, when one has observed the same smile under extraordinary circumstances, – in moments of pain, shame, disappointment, – that one becomes suspicious of it.'[7] The smile, when a Japanese has to convey refusal, means: 'I am sorry that I have to hurt you. My smile is intended to show respect for your feelings, and to soften the blow of disappointment which I, to my regret, have to impose on you.'

There is less popular devotion to larger units – the state for example, or the government. 'Government laws are only seven-day laws' is an old Japanese saying. (There is, of course, the Emperor. He is different, because he is Nation *and* Faith; because he incarnates, vaguely but deeply, the soul, not the body, of Japan.) And since devotion to distant power is weak, we should not be surprised that (essentially and excepting brand names like Gucci or Hermès for the rising middle classes) overseas nations rank low in interest to the Japanese.

One need not be surprised: 'abroad' does not play well in Peoria either; or in Manchester, Mainz, Marseilles and Milan. Or in New England, which is said to believe in the brotherhood of man, the fatherhood of God, and the neighbourhood of Boston.

Status and the Japanese

'Work' has a nobler connotation in Japan than in the West. A Japanese gets on with the job of building for the future, not because he has an exalted vision of it, but because he knows what has to be done today if there *is* to be a future. If the millenium can be reached (if it exists) he will try. If not, there is enough work to get on with. Like Voltaire's *Candide*, he knows that he must cultivate his communal garden.

Nemawashi is the term used by Japanese gardeners about the careful preparation necessary to transplant a bush, shrub or tree. The term is used metaphorically by commerce and industry as well. Since plants dislike being moved but since it is necessary to replant – meaning that one must keep up with the times – it is also necessary to prepare for the replanting carefully and together, which is a demonstration of the common Japanese tendency to relate the old to the new and to use parallels from actual or legendary history to make strange new things familiar.

The middle class has put the elite obligations of knightliness to work. With some exceptions, the accent in large Japanese companies is on certain but slow progression for employees. Safe in the knowledge that his status is secure, an employee is ready to accept changed assignments, perform new functions, be moved to new locations. Such readiness is a general hallmark of elites: members willingly submit to inconvenient service and yet regard such service honourable.

During the Heian dynasty of the late ninth to the twelfth centuries, 'the Japanese, in spite of their respect for the knowledge and wisdom of China and the privileges accorded to outstanding craftsmen, believed that in matters of government birth and descent came first.' By contrast, 'the Chinese believed that ability, and the successful passing of examinations, was necessary.'[8] Modern Japan has, however, reverted to the Chinese method. It is as essential for an aspiring Japanese to have attended universities like Tokyo or Keio as it is for an aspiring Frenchman to have been at a *grande école*. (But genius will out, and one is pleased to find that the founders of Honda, Matsushita Electric and others built great enterprises without academic certification.)

These were Japan's courtly, aristocratic centuries. Almost all land belonged to a few exalted families, who were themselves free of taxation. Disaffection with such egregious privilege led to the rise of a class of protesting samurai. They were to be the defining class of Japan until the middle of the nineteenth century.

In the seventeenth century, the Tokugawa shogunate secluded Japan hermetically. It applied knightly discipline – *bushido*, 'the warrior's way' – to the daily life of all classes. Discipline was given an extended meaning. The duty of fealty of the samurai knight to his lord was expanded to include loyalty by everyone to his superiors. There was strict definition of who was subservient to whom: servant to master, wife to husband, son to father, young to old. To make each man's status easily recognizable, even styles of clothing were prescribed; sumptuary laws limited expenditure.

The lord was under obligation to be protector and benefactor; the liege-man was under obligation to repay. But whereas the obligations of the lord were limited, the citizen's reciprocation was not. Reciprocation – the *On* of conventional obligation – could for the lord be full quittance, but not for him; there was always a running debit of obligation left in his account. The nearest Western analogue to *On* may well be the Christian understanding of Divine Grace: God grants His Grace to man; man cannot bestow grace on God; but man must always pray and praise Him.

But, also, learning and craftsmanship were honoured and encouraged by the samurai class. Learning was not greatly honoured by the merchant classes. And so the ancestry of large contemporary Japanese business lies in a samurai not a mercantile tradition. Its practical expression is in the recruitment from elite universities, its low emphasis on individualism, its high emphasis on collective endeavour, and its low emphasis on profit as an end in itself. In short, in non-mercantile means applied to mercantile ends.

Swords were made in ways that mingled fine metallurgy with *Shinto* religious ceremony. Houses were modular – standard *tatami* mat and window sizes being the modules. Precision, measurement, a tidiness of house and person, have long been part of Japanese artisanship – unlike Indian or Chinese arts and crafts which could rise to great beauty but, with a few exceptions, not precision. There was a diffuseness in their art which is absent in Japan. There was, furthermore, no tradition in Japan of tolerant forgiveness for failure, defeat, imperfect work or service. Here was a blend of disciplines to take Japan forward from 1868, the year of the Meiji Restoration and the ending of the Shogunates.

It may be true, as Alexis de Tocqueville claimed, that not 'a single people can be cited, since human history began, that has, of its own free will and by its own exertions, created an aristocracy within its bosom'. But Japan has chosen a knightly code for commercial business conduct – without an aristocracy. The British and the French, by contrast, were unable to resist the blandishments of high gentility – with poor effects on business progress. Knightliness worked in Japan because it was domesticated for daily use.

One must not suppose that knightly is the same as gentlemanly. Ninety per cent of the Japanese believe themselves to be of the middle class. A nation in which so great a number are of the middle category, but of which so many use a collective code of behaviour culled from chivalry, is a phenomenon unmatched by any other nation.

It was Sir Henry Maine's celebrated observation that in the course of the ages the respective duties and obligations of people in European society – masters and servants, rulers and subjects – ceased to be based on their status in society and moved to a relationship defined by contract. In Japan, even now, men's status *is* their contract.

Notes

1 Ivan Morris, *The World of the Shining Prince*, Peregrine, 1985, pp. 98–99.
2 G. B. Sansom, *Japan: A Short Cultural History* (1931), Stanford University Press, Stanford, 1952, pp. 468, 520, 522.
3 Lafcadio Hearn, *Japan: an Interpretation*, Macmillan, New York, 1904.
4 Shidzue Ishimoto, *Facing Two Ways*, Farrar & Rinehart, New York, 1935.
5 Miriam Beard, *A History of the Businessman*, Macmillan, New York, 1938.
6 R. H. Tawney, *Religion and the Rise of Capitalism*, John Murray, London, 1922; Max Weber, *The Protestant Ethic and the Spirit of Capitalism* (1904–5), ed. Talcott Parsons, 1930.
7 Lafcadio Hearn, *Glimpses of an Unfamiliar Japan*, Houghton, Mifflin, Cambridge, Mass., 1894.
8 C. V. Wedgwood, *The Spoils of Time*, Doubleday, New York, 1985.

14

Civility in Business Enterprise

Manners Maketh Man

Japan is an information society and has been one for many years. A rich palette of feelings and most possible forms of behaviour have been captured in the Japanese code of daily conduct – as expressed in ethics, gestures, forms of speech and etiquette.

Manners serve to make behaviour intelligible and prevent surprises. Manners are conventional signals, familiar to sender and recipient alike. A Japanese can understand another more perfectly than can a Westerner another, because manners speak more precisely than words; they are information beyond speech. In this sense Japanese civilization has richer sources than most others and needs few written agreements. A society – as, for example, the United States – in which a great many relationships have to be defined by contract, is a society in which an excess of definitions tends to overwhelm the general understanding.

And so, in a society in which mutual obligations are defined by common convention, information is easier to manage than in a society which requires special descriptions for every new relationship. In short, the Japanese need more lawyers than an Amazonian tribe, but far fewer than Americans. Japan is proof of the fact that if the very mind of a nation is an institution of common understanding there is less need for other institutions. And if we ask why Japanese managers serving their companies abroad are usually recalled home after three years, it is because so dense a culture needs a lot of maintenance.

At least in business, it is easier to understand the Japanese – easier than to understand businessmen of some other nations whose civilizations have retained a bazaar mentality and who hover between slyness, sudden greed and patient cunning. Still, the Japanese are not always pleased to be completely understood: it is a form of nakedness.

Lafcadio Hearn agreed that the Japanese ethical system was maintained to the extreme of giving fixity to ideas and at the cost of individuality. He did not think that it was favourable to originality. It tended to enforce an amiable mediocrity of opinion and imagination.

> Wherefore a foreign traveller in the interior cannot but long sometimes for the sharp, erratic inequalities of Western life, with its larger joys and pains and its more comprehensive sympathies . . . But . . . the intellectual loss is more than compensated by the social charm; and there can remain no doubt in the mind of one who even partly understands the Japanese, that they are still the best people in the world to live among.[1]

But, writing in 1904, he felt that Japan, faced with industrialization, would harden, lose her charm and morally decline. As described, it happened for a time.

She has lost some charm, has hardened in some respects, softened in others. Her values, in big business, have shifted. But to speak of a moral decline would be mistaken – the contrary might perhaps be claimed. What has happened is what is bound to happen when making money impinges on knightly values. The latter have had to yield a little to the reality of the other. Young managers live under the code but, with a fading memory of the past, tend to forget its origins. Most members of large Japanese trading companies do not know much of their country's past. Except as history sets the national mood, Japanese businessmen are not historically minded.

The transition from feudal rule to modern industrialism was at first – from about the 1890s to the 1920s – largely a tale of cruel disregard for human decency. All the elements for advancement were there: good artisans and a good apprenticeship tradition; labour contractors, *oyakata*, who had grown to the size of middling-to-big business from their own small beginnings as craftsmen, and who treated their labour as familially and well as circumstance permitted; European and American experts who taught the Japanese techniques and recommended decency; the existence of respectful Confucian family relationships; a labour force which was ready to give of itself. But, withal, a disregard by industry for any consequence of the degradation which it caused – fed by an excess of labour.

In 1911, the government lost patience and passed a Factory Act to regulate conditions, including those of women – young women – who had been bearing the heaviest burden of rapacity. Business resisted government, but had in the end to fight back with the only weapon likely to be effective against encroachment by the law: imitation. Deliberately, and with the blessings of a few enlightened philosopher-businessmen, it put its house in order and filled the new bottles of industrialization with the old wine of Japanese family tradition. It worked. The fact that meanwhile the *zaibatsu*, the giant conglomerations like Mitsui and Mitsubishi, had grown to power as ruling oligopolies, helped. They needed moderation and were prepared to pay for it.

In 1874, shortly after the ending of the Tokugawa era, Japan's exports were worth 200,000 dollars. Thirty years later they had grown a thousandfold; one hundred years later they had grown over three hundred thousandfold. Being diffident about their personal persuasiveness as salesmen, the Japanese achieved this remarkable record by the relatively obvious method of making products irresistible, good, cheap at the price, known and available.

Yet, also one hundred years from 1874, while in the United States each year approximately one 'residential unit' was built for every hundred inhabitants, only one for each six hundred inhabitants was built in Japan – disregarding the difference in the size of units. Even today, a Tokyo suburban three-bedroom house costs a middle-management worker his salary for about forty years, compared with about six years for an American in similar circumstances. (Given Japan's lower mortgage rates, the difference reduces to the equivalent of, say, twenty years to six.) Any young Japanese manager working at the head office of a major corporation will, at late dinner in a restaurant, diffidently admit that while he booked rich overseas orders that day, he would still have to travel from one to two hours in a crowded bus or by rail to a small home after his long working day and business dinner, and would tomorrow retrace the same long path

Civility in Business Enterprise

In Japan, the rules of precedence give manufacturers primacy of esteem over marketers; big corporations over small corporations; government departments over private businesses; old over young; higher rank over lower rank. Let a foreigner dare to estimate the appropriate depth for the customary bows in an encounter between the president of a manufacturing company of the second rank and a middle-aged director of a major trading corporation at the office of a departmental head in the Ministry of International Trade and Industry (MITI): he shall be considered brave. A stranger may not understand the proper dosing of the bow of greeting, but it is rarely unproportionate amongst the Japanese; at least, no Japanese complains of improper etiquette in this respect.

From this, it may be thought that Japan is still impenitently hierarchical. It is not so. Japan, so far as 'big' business and professional government are concerned, is a managerial union. The 'revolving door' – the transit of senior civil servants from government to private service, which is frowned upon in the United States – is a common one-way turnstile in Japan, and is blessed. Japanese civil servants bestow the honour of a 'descent from heaven', as they call it, to grace the management and boardrooms of great corporations by their presence.

The general rule is promotion according to length of service. As was remarked in a different context, 'there's no damned merit in it'. Generally, outstanding young performers receive no more rank, and little more reward, than average performers. Surprisingly – impossibly by Western standards of ambition – they are prepared to accept this in the knowledge that their reward will come when they reach 50 and become directors of their company whilst others just serve out their term.[2] This, it is said, is changing, but the change is slow and still exceptional.

Mid-career managers are expected to understand their company's broad interest, and to recommend detailed policy. Senior managers pass careful judgement on it, but rarely veto it. Indeed, if a senior manager wishes to suggest a certain course, he is likely to call one of the line-managers and acquaint him with his thoughts. The line-manager will then make the proposal in the written form called a *ringisho*, as though he were originator of the thought, and pass it up the line until it goes back to where it started; and there it will, of course, be approved. The actual proponent may take no credit – with modesty unthinkable in the West.

Since all proposals undergo extensive scrutiny, there is no point in being clever in Japan. Things are best stated as they are. If they fit into the scheme of things or are wisely made to fit they will speak for themselves. If not, a reputation for being very cunning will be the sum of all achievement. Since lower ranks provide the burden of decisions, it is proper and more fruitful in the end for a foreigner to make his first proposals to the man-in-charge, rather than to top management. Let the section or department head take them up to his superiors for their seal. If the matter is worthwhile, it will be sure to float up to the top in properly digested form. The *ringi* system of decision-making is under critical scrutiny, but it has not so far been replaced.

Japan is a union of managers, by managers, and for the perpetuation of the managerial system of Japan. The managers are wise enough to know that workers' and citizens' consent has a price which must be paid. They are also aware of the fact that citizens' savings are the source of future investments. It helps them to know that the personal savings rate is four times greater in Japan than in the USA, and they are certain to want to keep it that way (even though it may no longer be in Japan's wider interest). Everyone knows where power lies inside the system and where each stands: power lies with managers and none but managers report to other managers. Owners are rarely seen. Is this system of managerial predominance good or bad? That depends on how one wishes to answer George Will's contention that the 'question is always which elites shall rule, not whether elites shall rule'.[3]

In practice, ownership has less operational meaning in Japan than in the West. Ownership is widely diffused: share-holding is disseminated between banks and affiliated corporations – many having some interest in the other. Small dividends on percentually small profits is not of overriding importance to the bank which has an equity interest in a *keiretsu* (such major trade-and-industry groups as Mitsui, Mitsubishi or Sumitomo), because the total equity may be from four to some thirty times less than the capital employed – incredible by Western standards. The bank, as a major lender to the group, enjoys the flow of vast interest payments more than relatively meagre dividends. Profits by trading corporations, for example, are from one-third of one per cent to four-tenths of a per cent of sales – inadequate by Western standards. (But at a loan-to-equity ratio of 30 to 1, and a profit on sales of one-third per cent, the return on equity is fully 10 per cent before tax – more than adequate in a country with low interest rates.)

The essence of Japan's commercial philosophy is to keep the country going, to keep people employed and to allow investments and modernization to continue. By this means, Japan has turned Marx's critique of capitalism against Marx himself. Marx contended that the capitalist skims the surplus value for his, the capitalist's, own benefit. So, on the face of it, does the Japanese capitalist, but with a twist that Marx did not foresee: he did not foresee that Japanese corporations would immediately turn the money back into investments for the further benefit of managers and employees.

Those who would have Western industry adopt the Japanese method of management should consider that the above sketch contains one impossible, one unthinkable, one inadequate, and one incredible; in all, one great un-imitable. Impossible: to wait for decades for merited promotion. Unthinkable: to use the same obscure decision path. Incredible: to accept so high a corporate loan-to-equity ratio. Inadequate: for shareholders and managements to be satisfied with so small a percentage of profits on total sales.

That which can and should be imitated – low interest rates, modern machines and manufacturing methods; planning; good product; efficiency; 'quality circles' (a pre-1930 Ford invention); international marketing and distribution – is what the West preached to Japan in the first place. The pupil remembered, the teacher began to forget.

The Westering of Japan

Japan's success is primarily more a social than a technological phenomenon.

Instead of seeing in the catastrophe of a lost war a final loss of hope, the Japanese saw in it a first step in reconstruction. The economist Keynes asked 'by what means it is right and reasonable to call on the living generation to restrict their consumption, so as to establish, in course of time, a state of full investment for their successors'.[4] Japan has so far given him a successful though disproportionate answer.

Japan's socio-industrial structure enabled her to concentrate on major 'tractor' industries and institutions, not unlike the concentration of talent and capital in chosen parts of the Soviet economy. But far from perfectly: secondary and tertiary industries in Japan are still rarely as effective or as profitable as the leaders. There, 'bottom-to-top' decision-making yields to the Western style: the boss gives orders.

Lifetime security of employment in them is rare or non-existent. Nor is domestic distribution a model for the world. It is expensive and restrictive, just as it is in Switzerland, another island *sui generis* and the only country in Western Europe which equally resists changes in her peaceful and stable ways, and which has equally managed to maintain full employment, high savings and low interest rates (and which also has a native form of *sumo* wrestling). There is scarcely a consumer article or food which is cheaper in Japan than in the USA or Britain, Germany and France. This includes many mass-produced things with which Japan has conquered the world. Japanese cameras or electronic devices are cheaper in the USA than in Japan – just as Swiss gold-encrusted watches are cheaper off Fifth Avenue in New York than on the Bahnhofstrasse in Zürich.

One may note that in this age, when manufacturing is said to be shrinking in relation to services, Japan's international success has been almost entirely a triumph of manufacturing. Her service industries have not, so far, been eminent contributors to her international growth. This, too, will change.

In the late forties, when Europe and Japan were emerging from their condition of miserable ruin; when the United States was the world's only source of succour, money and supplies; when her balance of trade with the rest of the world was highly in her favour; when the dollar was 'hard' and all other moneys 'soft', the commonest examination question at schools of economics was how the world's economy could cope with permanent indebtedness to the USA. It was a question that had no answer then. But within fifteen years the great reversal was complete: the dollar, adamantine before, assumed the hardness of a coddled egg. Today the Japanese balance-of-trade surplus with the United States alone is equal to, or greater than, Saudi Arabia's entire gross domestic product twelve or so years ago.

The West and Japan will borrow from each other. But, contrary to a common view, the West has less, not more, to borrow from Japan than Japan must borrow from the West. Japan is the first country which has proved conclusively that Western industrial civilization is universal. The westering of Japan is more significant than her remaining easterliness.

Some things, clearly, have happened and will continue to happen; there will be more foreign investment in Japan; far more foreign investment by Japan; more joint investments with the Japanese, both in Japan herself and elsewhere; lower interest rates everywhere. But we cannot copy everything: we cannot copy 'depression cartels' as in Japan because they are forbidden by law; we cannot use high financial leverage (gearing) by industry and commerce, whereby a dollar owned is enhanced by eight to thirty dollars borrowed – our banks will not, quite rightly, assume such risks; we cannot copy Japanese 'orderly marketing' because it is legally sanctioned oligopoly.

Japan, on the other hand, in this converging world, will by degrees surrender some of her remaining commercial quaintnesses and much of her self-containedness. Japanese capital is moving to other countries, not for commercial advantage alone, but also because many Japanese corporations are losing patience with their own bureaucracy. Japan's watchdog, MITI, will lose much of its control. Japanese industry is also moving overseas because insufficient opportunities for expansion remain in her domestic market – now a market of considerable but slowing growth, and with high savings still. What emigrant Japanese horticulture has achieved in Brazil, emigrant Japanese industry can achieve in other countries – but with imponderable effects on its own soul. To be sure, Japanism will remain for domestic comfort. But the Easternness of Japan is a non-renewable resource, while the Westernness she has adopted still grows like dragons' teeth.

No competition is as fierce as that between Japanese corporations. This has been a major factor in her success: she had no need to be concerned about her efficiency compared with foreign competitors. Competition had done the job domestically before foreign competitors had ever joined the contest. She need not fear foreign competition, need not seek autarky, need not discourage imports: domestic competition will continue to serve her more fully than protectionism.

Her high educational and training standards allow her to apply a higher management density to industrial processes. While Western talent is as great and occasionally greater than hers, it is often applied intermittently, instead of continuously, as in Japan. A study of several dozen companies in the USA and in Japan that use robots, concluded that rather than narrowing the gap with Japan, the technology of automation is widening it further.'[5] American manufacturers failed to exploit the flexibility of the systems and did not show the same degree of production 'literacy' as Japanese manufacturers.

As Japan's trade surpluses continue, they will become more a problem for herself than for others. Indeed, they *have* become more a problem for herself than others. Beyond a point, overwhelming superiority in certain manufactured goods is an invitation to catastrophic retaliation. Her fears, despite all evidence to the contrary, that she is poor and must save money; her obsession with dependency on foreign food and raw materials; her mercantilist, self-protective disposition; even her sense of isolation and otherness – all these must fade before the new realities.

One of these realities is that she has irreversibly become a member in good standing of the club of industrial nations. Her condition has changed from a need to accumulate to a need to enjoy the fruits of accumulation. She, above all other nations, must seek the freest trade and must in the long run buy from others as much as she sells to others – or give away her surplus in foreign aid.

The alternative, even without retaliation by other nations, is fateful: if Japan accumulates in trading surpluses and savings more than she can domestically absorb, she must continue to invest these surpluses abroad. In reasonable measure this is to her and the world's good. But in excess she will find herself the owner of much of the rest of the world – owner in all but sovereignty, and thus at other sovereigns' mercies. And thus her dilemma: her continuing large surpluses-in-trade will be a sword inverted against herself. It would indeed be a disservice to history if Japan, for all her vision, were to stumble from short-sightedness.

There is a hurdle that Japan must jump before her future becomes secure. It is a hurdle that she may not be able to jump, because the hurdle is her own shadow. Japan is an alliance of competing lobbies. Her government is a part of this alliance, but not an overwhelming part. Big business, the *keiretsu*, are a part, but not an overwhelming part. Farmers, consumers, small industry, are likewise a part, but not an overwhelming part.

The whole adds up to a body politic whose limbs insist on their own unchanging ways. The civil service, the bureaucrats, cannot help protecting exports and dissuading imports. They cannot help being patriotic, just as civil services anywhere are always patriotic. Japan knows, as everyone knows, that the present flood of uncompensated exports must abate. But it is not in the nature of the Japanese system to cause pain to its constituents. Whereas wisdom would require Japan to solve her problem, she cannot easily do so from within. And so it may be the despairing action (or its threat) of her customer-countries, the USA and Europe, which may have to force her. As it turns out, since the above was written, their threatening despair has made her begin to see and seek new ways; and she has not yet forgotten that the United States has been her consistent friend for forty years – so far perhaps the only genuine friend she has had among the nations.

Japan's communal and social ideals are not an imitable model for the world. She gained her present strength from hard work and from trade in the open markets of the world. She can enhance her influence through the needs of other nations, but not through their natural sympathies. She has not given the world a revolutionary ideal of human values; not an American revolutionary ideal of individual rights; not a French revolutionary ideal of social equality; not even revolutionary socialist visions. Japan's is a life of high civility; but is not a civility to inspire longing dreams in other nations. To let herself be seen as a great power of friendly intent she may have to continue to walk arm-in-arm with the United States, whose own model may be flawed but still has many friends.

The world's truth is changing for her. She is no longer an outsider, and knows it.

On being engaged to marry the Baron Ishimoto in the early part of this century, Shidzue had to provide a bridal trousseau to last her for life. She listed it in over ten pages of her reminiscences: 10 ceremonial kimonos for winter, 4 ceremonial kimonos for spring and autumn, 8 ceremonial kimonos for summer, 117 other kimonos for various seasons, 27 'petticoat' kimonos for various seasons, 35 *haori*-coats and overcoats, 39 ceremonial and other *obis* (ornamental waist sashes) and hundreds of other items. In Japan today, many brides will have worn a ceremonial kimono for the first time in their lives.

Notes

1 Lafcadio Hearn, *Glimpses of an Unfamiliar Japan*, Houghton, Mifflin, Cambridge, Mass., 1894.
2 In Japan, at over 50, unsuccessful managers will be given a desk by a window, a daily newspaper to read and no responsibilities. In Germany, the equivalent of the Japanese 'man by the window' is the 'man far away from a window' – '*weit weg vom Fenster*'.
3 George Will, *Statecraft as Soulcraft*, Simon & Schuster, New York, 1983.
4 J. M. Keynes, *The General Theory of Employment Interest and Money*, Macmillan, London, 1936.
5 Ramchandran Rajkumar, 'Postindustrial Manufacturing', *Harvard Business Review*, Oct–Nov. 1986.

PART III

Future

Section 6
Business in the Age of Information

Preamble

Tools help man do work he cannot do unaided, but they mostly do the work that man, given enough time, can do. To this, the class of machines we call computers is not yet an exception. But man is to an extent also a tool of his tools; they set the pace and nature of his work. They transform the way nations live. By this means they change the quality of societies and organizations.

Tools and powered machines eliminated much of man's sweat and labour. They substituted machine skills for many manual skills. By holding, sorting and retrieving information, they now substitute memory. They give new forms to archives and libraries and extend these forms to business. They determine the sequencing of work-flows and the choice of consequential actions. They are fast, tidy and precise beyond man's ability. These are matters examined in this section.

But while computers greatly change the nature of organizations, they do not change individual nature, ambitions and intentions to the same extent – because they deal with work, not values. Computers open new entrepreneurial avenues, but they do not create entrepreneurs. Computers help to judge, but they are not, except in a simple and mechanical sense, themselves judges. Wisdom is still ours – sometimes; wisdom is not theirs – ever.

The present half-century has seen changes in business and the world economy which will carry us into the next century. The greatest of these changes has been the new meanings given to the classical, late eighteenth-century economic theory of the international division of labour, a theory which advocated the global benefits of letting each country supply to others, without let or hindrance, that which it could most cheaply produce.

The theory now redefines itself in several ways. Beside the 'cheapest' division, the international division of labour, we now have an international division of management effectiveness, an international division of fashion preferences, an international division of quality preferences and an international division of currency and interest-rate preferences. Japan's success, for example, has been mainly one of international division of management effectiveness.

Since the Second World War, global trade has increased more than fivefold. On average, about one-fifth of all the wealth produced by the world is traded between nations, and the best trading partners of the world's advanced economies are other advanced economies with a similar palette of products. The preference that, say, American or British consumers sometimes show for, say, foreign cars is a manifestation of an international division of fashion preferences, and not a need for cars.

It is sometimes also a manifestation of the international division of quality preferences. National standards of quality have deep historical roots. Generally, countries in which a product started as a luxury for the few, but whose consumption has now permeated to common use, have higher standards than countries in which the products were made for common consumption from the beginning. There were the mechanical watches and chocolates of Switzerland, English teas, woollens and hunting guns, the porcelains and silks of France, the laces and tapestries of Belgium, all of which were initially made for princely courts, for the nobility and for the rich. It was the rich, not the masses, who determined the character of goods. Their demand was for lovely things, for things to last a lifetime. Traditions of quality also came from countries with a history of apprenticeship.

Such was not the case in the United States. In 1839, Alexis de Tocqueville 'met an American sailor, and asked him why his country's ships are made so that they will not last long. He answered offhand that the art of navigation was making such quick progress that even the best of boats would almost be useless if it lasted more than a few years.' De Tocqueville recognized 'in these casual words of an uneducated man ... the general and systematic conception by which a great people conducts its affairs'.[1]

There is, last, the international division in currency and interest-rate preferences. Financial fundamentals have become irrelevant in daily business. Fluctuations in the price of currencies *on any given day* cannot be related to fundamentals. The bribe of high interest rates which one country offers in competition with another determines the demand for money – not to attract trade in merchandise, but to attract trade in its own money-as-commodity.

Another major change is spurred by the application of computers to production and services. If robotization is instituted badly, it only serves to increase rigidity and capital cost. But if it is done well and eliminates labour, it also eliminates the importance of wage rates: it no longer matters whether the prevailing wage rate is twenty dollars per hour, or only five; if no labour is used, the cost of labour is zero. Three major consequences flow from this: the first is that other factors dominate – such as overheads and the cost of borrowed money in a given country compared with another. The second is that robotization works to the disadvantage of under-industrialized countries: if direct labour cost tends to descend to zero in highly developed economies, the Third World no longer offers any special favour to investments. The third consequence is that it makes the international division of management effectiveness doubly important.

Advance came at those times and to those nations whose high savings and high investments were conjoined with educated and venturesome managements and workers. Scientific and industrial research, and research for purposes of its industrial application, still matter: they generate more information, and certainly more knowledge, than all the world's computers yoked together.

But while technology matters, it is not technological leadership alone that matters. Like water, technology is fungible and flows. Scientific knowledge moves and escapes with the speed of light from one country's good minds to another's. Not technology alone, but its wise, brave and massive application makes the strength of nations. That is the implied subject of this section.

Note

1 Alexis de Tocqueville, *Democracy in America*, 1839, vol. 1, part 1, ch. 8.

15

People, Computers and Business

Computers and Business

Computers are not yet an alternative life-form. For the time being they are peculiar and non-traditional tools. Computers are limited but infinite machines, whereas man's mind is unlimited but finite. Computers are definite machines, whereas man is an indefinite machine. Man is diffuse, but computers have hard edges. Therefore, computers are not given to metaphysics, but man is a speculative animal and asks questions he has not been invited to ask.

The earliest critical remarks about computing machines – certainly the first critical remarks from America – were made by Oliver Wendell Holmes, author of *The Autocrat of the Breakfast Table*, in 1858. This remarkably quick transition from a drawing board in England to a literary dinner table in New England concerned Charles Babbage's 'difference engine', built some twenty years earlier, in England. The difference engine was only a calculator, but Babbage had also designed a great 'analytical engine' in the same decade. This was to have been a mechanical computer, encompassing all the elements of its modern electronic counterpart. Had it been completed, the world might have begun to use engineered computers, as against human computers, a century before it did.

It was not completed for lack of money. Private firms saw no use in it. With the extraordinary exception of the Duke of Wellington, Napoleon's adversary and a soldier-statesman who was turned out of office too early to continue his support of Babbage, British government ministers neither understood the purpose of the engine, nor did they have the imagination to recognize Babbage's genius.

But Babbage's attempts had another effect. He needed remarkable accuracy in the turning and shaping of the parts for his engines – an accuracy of which British industry had hitherto been incapable. He designed the necessary machine tools himself and sought out those few able mechanics in England who could make them. Such close-tolerance machine tools gave Britain an advantage over continental European engineering. In this way Babbage not only served computer science in the twentieth century, but also helped to create his country's mechanical triumphs in the nineteenth.

Oliver Wendell Holmes was neither mathematician nor engineer, but professor of anatomy and physiology at Harvard. He had heard only of the first of Babbage's engines, the calculator. He said it was 'a Frankenstein-monster, a thing without brains and without heart, too stupid to make a blunder; that turns out results like a cornsheller, and never grows any wiser or better, though it grind a thousand bushels of them.'

Holmes had it right: computers are too stupid to make blunders and computers are not wise. But what tools these are – never to blunder, and never to pretend to wisdom; never to know the difference between game and reality; never to know the difference between actual truth and falsehood; but always to know the difference between logical truth and falsehood.

Meeting a Computer

The owner-manager of a small business bought a small computer in the early seventies. This made him an early user of personal computers for business purposes. It was a Hewlett-Packard 9815A, the size of a briefcase, with a built-in strip printer and magnetic tape cassette, and only 2,000 bytes of internal memory. But the files in the cassette could be chained together and could be loaded successively by a 'load-and-go' command, whereby one file would automatically call up the next one. This allowed him to make programs 50,000 bytes long, including many data. It was a facility he liberally used.

Programs ran slowly by the standards of today, and it took some minutes to go through a long and many-filed operation which a modern machine would do in seconds. Still, that was less than the hour it would have taken to do the calculations by slide rule (in case anyone still remembers slide rules); less than by using one of those little cranking devices now no longer seen, with a little bell in them to tell one when one had cranked too far; less also than by using a hand-held electronic calculator.

It was not designed for data bases; but together they created data bases. It was not designed to operate with alphabetic strings of characters; but together they learned to cheat and to operate with a limited alphabetic capability. It went round the world with him more than a dozen times. He learned a great deal about the limits of his own intelligence – largely humility. It was anything but 'user-friendly', but it was, well, a friend.

He also learned the difference between programming and use. When he was programming he had to think the way the computer 'thinks'; when he used it, he had to do as he had told it to make him do. There is a great deal of difference between the two activities: in programming, one is almost the master; in using the program, almost the obedient servant – a fact which turns out to have remarkable consequences in business when those who design the programs are not the same people who must use them. It conveyed a sense of power to the point of fascination: fascination with the way it jumped all the hurdles of conditions, loops and hoops; the way it knew the location of any datum tucked away in hidden little corners within a slowly written program; the way it did this with speed and ease and even elegance. It was as though his poorly and painfully constructed sequences were transformed by an intellectual wit far greater than its author's.

It helped him to make money. At a rough guess, the net after-tax return on the 3,000 dollar investment was between 20,000 and 30,000 per cent – if the calculation is admissible without the inclusion of its partner, the owner-programmer-operator. The machine is still with him – out to pasture like its owner. He wrote a good number of programs for it and cannot, alas, transfer them to another machine; it was not built with that facility. So he will keep it and recall old times.

It is necessary, in the interests of accuracy, to add that investments subsequently made in larger computers yielded him only a fraction – a negative fraction at times – of these percentages.

Computers and Eternity

Programs are in a sense eternal. This seems to distinguish computer software from other inventions of man. Like civilization itself, there is no limit to what can be added to it. Little need be wasted. Write a word-processing program, for example, as a core. Add to it a dictionary to check the spelling of the words. Add to it a syntactical and grammatical analyser to check the text for orthodoxy. Add to it voice recognition, so that one can speak and say 'insert the word "word" after the words "insert the",' instead of using keys. Add to it a translation program, so one can say 'translate this text into colloquial Japanese.' Add to it a voice synthesizer, so one can say 'read me the Japanese translation in a woman's voice,' and then 'type it out in *katakana* characters.' Add to it a cryptographic screen to hide this immortal prose from vulgar eyes. Add to it printers and compositors to put the text in column form on designated pages. Add to it the ability to send the text to distant places at great speed. The core program module remains through all concatenations. Some of the above abilities exist; others are about to come.

We cannot do this with novels, poems, paintings, pots, pans or pencil-sharpeners: to expand these is to change them. Many other works of man are subject to decay, but not, at least in principle, software. Essentially it can reside, refreshable, for ever. It is the first product men have devised which has some measure of eternity: it is not consumed by use. If there is a limit to the life of software, it arises not from its own functioning, but from changes in hardware technology or of operating systems. One would be as reluctant to replace an old computer with good software on which much work has been done as one would be to replace an experienced and energetic old manager.

The mid-nineteenth-century writer Ruskin did not enjoy the romantic habit of other poets, such as Tennyson, of giving animals and flowers human sentiments: roses weeping, larkspurs listening, lilies whispering, now the crimson petal sleeping, now the white. Ruskin called it the 'pathetic fallacy'. The computer is our new pathetic fallacy. We somehow endow it with an *élan vital* of its own, a vital energy beyond the flow of electrons or photons.

It has always been a human habit to animate unthinking things – stones, rivers, trees, fire, forests – with spirit: to keep us company, and yet to awe us a little. It would be hard to think of more unlikely candidates for such endowment than the sorting machines we call computers. And yet, we find it almost impossible not to speak of the computer without words used of the working of a mind. We say 'it thinks', and subconsciously add 'therefore it is' (even though that, as a friend remarked, is putting Descartes before the horse).

We could compare the computer with one of our many metabolic organs, but we insist on comparing it with the mind, perhaps by an analogy with silence; the computer, like the mind, does not appear to feed or to eliminate; it does not contract or expand like the beating of a heart; it does not sweat or sigh. It is silent when it works; just as is the milling of the mind when it thinks in solitude.

Computers and Information

The age of knowledge-based or information-based society is said to have arrived. It is not the first time. We note, as a minor reflection on human nature, that Adam and Eve caused the Fall of Man from an excess of eagerness for knowledge. As Genesis 3:6 tells us, they ate of 'a tree to be desired to make one wise'. They did not eat of it, as one might suppose, to indulge in lust, gluttony, envy, sloth or any of these.

We are still a long way from being a knowledge-based society. It could even be argued that tribal lives – lives close to the smells and moods of nature, lives of intimate relationships – are closer to their reality than the lives of businessmen are to their own. Their awareness of reality is confined to narrow and particular professional segments.

But was there ever any commerce not based on knowledge and information? Leave aside for the moment that information and knowledge are not the same. Knowledge cannot exist without information, but the availability of information is no guarantee of knowledge.

No decent joiner ever held a plane who did not know the construction of a chair and no worthy blacksmith ever lived who did not know the temper of his iron. The pyramids were not built with any lack of knowledge of levers, levels, lifts, windlasses, hoists, some astronomy and enough mathematics to have gauged the value of pi to within six parts per thousand of its reading today, 4,500 years later.

No good merchant in recorded history ever traded with success who did not know his products, their procurement, their price and markets. Before the Common Era, Phoenican sailor-merchants spread the goods, arts and sciences of the ancient world – its metals, dyes and manufactures – throughout the Mediterranean and as far as the Britannic islands; they retailed papyrus everywhere and used it for alphabetic writing to record their trades. The Greeks called books by the name of the great Phoenican city Byblos, and from this we derive the words 'bible' and 'bibliography'. The same Phoenicians were shrewd enough to sell olive oil to the Iberians in exchange for silver – more silver than their ship could carry in its holds. To carry the surplus away, they simply and cunningly replaced the ship's stone anchors with anchors made of solid silver.

Florentine bankers, such as the Medici of the fourteenth century, had twenty-four branches in France, thirty-seven in the kingdom of Naples, fifty in Turkey alone, and many more elsewhere. The accounts and reports of all these branches were sent to their head office in Florence for annual inspection.

The Hanseatic league in the fourteenth and fifteenth centuries had branches and offices from Norway and Russia to Venice, from London and Flanders to the cities of the Rhine: surveying, reporting, weighing and jealously maintaining their trading privileges.

The House of Rothschild had runners and riders bringing news of victories and defeats abroad before governments knew of them. Under the laws existing in the early to middle nineteenth century, the Frankfurt, London and Paris Rothschilds had to be separately incorporated. But by exchange of information, by consolidated annual (but, of course, not public) financial statements and by partnership agreements, all three main offices were as one. The Rothschilds were one of the first multinational corporations in the world, with branches and agencies in Vienna and Naples, Brussels, Madrid, New York, New Orleans, Havana, Mexico, Rome, Turin and Trieste. Between 1815 and 1863, their consolidated capital grew from 3.3 million to 558 million francs – an unequalled annual cumulative rate of 11.28 per cent, sustained for nearly half a century.

In London, in 1875, Lionel Rothschild knew enough to be able to raise four million pounds sterling *within hours*, to enable the British Government to buy a sizeable parcel of shares (but, contrary to popular belief, less than a majority) in the Suez Canal. This sum would now be the equivalent of between one half and one billion dollars. Major banks today have more information than the London Rothschilds. Whether they have more knowledge is an open question. But that they could not raise an equivalent sum in a few hours may be taken for granted, even if only because their legal departments would not allow them to act forthwith, as then, on a handshake and an oral promise, even of a president or prime minister.

The truth is that despite the flood of information, one has yet to meet the banker who is not himself overwhelmed by it. The wise old Swiss who started his working life as a Warburg banker and later created one of the world's largest pharmaceutical concerns, concluded that 'banks no longer know what they are doing,' and may be right.

What was it that the Rothschilds, the Fuggers, the Medici had (and all good merchants always had) that made them successful? Information, certainly. Certainly control. Most certainly, reputation. But not these three alone. Their most valuable resource was connections, correspondents, business friendships. There are, indeed, too many businessmen today who are too greatly bemused by the idea of streams of statistical and electronic information as a substitute for personal connections. The error may arise from reasoning which argues, consciously or otherwise, that the purpose of business connections is information, and that if the information is available on computer screens or telexes, there is no further need to waste one's time with people; that decisions can be taken on the basis of facts and trends, and that these suffice. Not yet so; facts are too lean; they lack the counterpoint of personal encounter. Facts by themselves lack consequences; despite the wealth of media news, nations still maintain smiling ambassadors abroad.

The best advice one can give to young business people is to cultivate wise human sources. It is from them, and not from data alone, that one learns an indispensable set of facts which are otherwise unavailable: how they judge and what they intend. Because what they intend today is likely to become tomorrow's market. To neglect connections in favour of non-human sources of information alone is to become a technical manipulator. This is particularly so when the information is not information at all but a set of instructions – elaborate but definite commands to make certain obligatory responses: if so, do this; if not so, do the other. One cannot acquire full knowledge of corporations from their published accounts and balance sheets; there are people in them who are unstated future assets or liabilities.

Computers and Knowledge

An absence of knowledge is weakness but knowledge is not always power. If knowledge were synonymous with power, we would be ruled by scholars and accountants. But we know that the world has more often been ruled by force and brutality than by brains and philosophy. Information is not power either, unless it leads to knowledge, and knowledge is not power unless it leads to judgement – and control.

We live, to be sure, in an age of information. The world is full of it. But if by knowledge is meant the wise use of information, one cannot be fully persuaded that we live in an age of knowledge – especially in business.

There are three kinds of information in business, which, for want of better terms, we may call accelerated information, enabling information and productive information. Accelerated information is the ability to produce, say, a financial statement quickly by means of suitable computer programs. Enabling information is the ability to run, say, the booking system of an airline. Both are valuable (and the latter extremely valuable) but neither necessarily means that the corporation's financial statement will be good or that the airline will prosper. It is the third kind, productive information, whatever its source, in which the arts of management reside, which helps good business conduct and leads to good decisions. It is information which is not automatic (like a financial statement or airline booking) but needs the intervention of a wise interpreter. It is the only kind of information which has meaning, if by meaning we mean information with consequences.

'Progress' is hardly worth the name if it leads to more computer printouts, more committee reports and nowhere in particular. Time and time again, men have attempted to design computer programs based on economic fundamentals in order to forecast currency exchange movements and fluctuations in the price of stocks and bonds. Time and time again, they have had to admit that they failed in this, and have had to fall back on the analysis of historical pointers: Januaries either good or bad, Aprils either cruel or kind, Fridays either lively or quiet, Monday mornings either favourable or unfavourable – one cannot remember which.

A recent (19 October 1987) precipitous drop in equity values on the New York Exchange came about partly this way: computers were programmed to signal 'trigger points' – points when forward, as against actual, prices of stocks reversed; the computers, in such an event, were to give a buy or sell signal. The purpose was to provide the team that ran the program with a differential advantage over the rest of the market. Each team hoped to have the signal first, buy or sell accordingly and make a profit (or prevent a loss) before the rest of the market realized what was happening. But because many teams had equally able computers, the same or similar signals came to all of them at the same time. All acted from information but not from understanding. The result was that the market fell; all had outguessed all. In other words, none had outguessed any and none had been in control. The failed technique, ironically, was sometimes called 'portfolio insurance'.

Knowledge is not quite the same thing as this kind of uniformly trivial awareness. If proliferation of information is all that computers and data networks manage to achieve in the world of money, then a growth of fewer and fewer secure financial instruments and of more and more mutually self-cancelling financial strategies is all we shall have gained from expensive machinery 'that turns out results like a cornsheller, and never grows any wiser or better, though it grind a thousand bushels of them'. Used irrationally, the uses of the computer, that most rational of instruments, become arcane and ruinous experiments in numerology.

Information is not a good in itself. Stripped of its mystique and 'high-tech' pretensions, information becomes little more than transmission. In the welter of such transmission information is included which is never even read, too much irrelevant information, too little relevant information, memoranda whose purpose is less to inform than to make one's presence felt, propaganda, covert advertising, malevolent information, disinformation, gossip and lies. We know, as Francis Bacon did, that knowledge is power; do we know, as Socrates did, that knowledge is virtue?

We need not be excessively pleased with a society which prides itself on the quantity of information it generates and the sophisticated ways in which it disseminates it, when we remember that certain types of information – music and concerts, publicly endowed and supported radio and television, pure and applied long-term scientific research and above all good education – are indifferently or poorly funded forms of information.

An information society is not of itself a new or better civilization. As far as business is concerned, prettily tabulated information is a satisfying form of neatness. But how much neatness do we need beyond that which maintains order and understanding? No industry has more information than, for example, banks. Yet their use of clerical labour is more abundant now than before the massive application of computers.

An inverse relationship may indeed exist between the amount of information on the one hand and courageous decisions on the other. There is now, for example, a great fund of detailed information for economic forecasting, but economic decision-making on a national let alone international scale is often less resolute now than in the past. Information entails cooperation – but whereas we have more of the former we have, at best, only the same amount of the latter. Nor does one often meet great pioneers among large corporations now.

And in a wider social context, there is 'nothing that we do not know about our cities – except how to make them quiet, clean, safe, and beautiful'.[1]

Computers and Being

If the question did not promise to become relevant to business at some date in the next two or three decades, we would not have to ask whether computers are merely tools or a new class of intelligent beings. Man has always been as much a tool of his tools as their master. But there have never been tools such as computers – tools that do the work *and* supervise their operators.

Like all machines, the class of machines known as computers have abilities but no intentions. The question is not whether computers think, or do not think, *by* themselves. It is whether computers think *for* themselves and on their own behalf. They are filters, screens and sieves so far; filing systems and data stores; work sequence controllers, categorizers, differential diagnosticians, calculators and so on. There is a class of programs that simulates understanding, asks questions, interprets them, selects the next relevant question and then, having gathered a number of pointers, chooses an answer from a finite fund of answers. It is the class of software known as 'artificial intelligence' and 'expert systems'. But, though purposeful, these programs are still only procedural intelligences. Computers 'think' by themselves but not for themselves. Theirs is thinking unattended by anybody, least of all themselves.

It is still we, not our computers, who must make decisions and seize opportunities. Just as we still feel, in the larger framework of affairs, that a human agent should make the decisions in matters of defence, rather than have them made by a battle-machine, so nothing is likely to replace fundamental human judgement for many years – because computers do not yet possess that great sink of general awareness which is the human mind.

The poet Byron's daughter, Ada Lovelace (after whom the computer language ADA is named), held similar opinions nearly a century and a half ago. She said, speaking of Charles Babbage's analytical engine, or mechanical computer, that it has no pretensions to originate anything: 'It can do whatever we know how to order it to perform.' In 1976, an eminent computer scientist could only agree with Ada Lovelace: 'Since we do not now have any ways of making computers wise, we ought not now give computers tasks that demand wisdom.'[2]

One could conceive of a computer connected to fine robotic manipulators playing the gigue from Bach's Third Cello Sonata consummately on a fine old instrument. One would not applaud it for a reason: not because it could not have done it well. But from indifference: a machine that cannot discriminate between playing J. S. Bach and 'Pop Goes the Weasel' is no sorcerer, not even a sorcerer's apprentice. Not that 'Pop Goes the Weasel' is a bad tune; 'Pop Goes the Weasel' is an admirable tune; but one ought to know the difference.

The question whether machines will at some future time think, is, in a sense, the same question as whether they will live. Notwithstanding the comment made above, we must ask the question specifically because machines may, one day, be able to run a business on their own. The signs are with us already: it is not too farfetched to imagine an airline booking system that needs no clerks; or a bank that needs no human intervention for a large category of transactions; or a financial investment service that selects the proper investment instruments for any client, and transacts the purchase or sale chosen by the client on its expert advice. Business is, to an extent, a sort of game bounded by rules of conduct and usage. Computers already play some very superior games, and can be similarly bound by rules of conduct and good usage.

It happened this way: Frankenstein Inc., Brokers in Foreign Exchange, was a corporation wholly owned by Dr Frankenstein, a bachelor with no family or relatives, himself a doctor of mathematics and the capable programmer of a very capable and large computer owned by the company. At the age of 65, Dr Frankenstein decided to retire. He could not find a capable enough successor – nor did he need one. He sold the company to its operating staff, the computer, by a management buy-out, including all the company's liabilities and assets. Dr Frankenstein's only major stipulations were: 1) the corporation would pay him half the profits for ten years or his lifetime, whichever was the lesser term, and 2) after his death the corporation was to become an eleemosynary foundation, that is to say, a foundation for non-profit, charitable purposes.

Frankenstein's computer, capable both of speech recognition and speech synthesis, and able to carry on a polite and businesslike telephone conversation with customers and sellers on the lines of ELIZA – a program originally designed to discuss with patients their mental states – and connected to external data bases which gave it all the latest results of all the exchanges in the world, competently continued business; it billed, collected payments, deposited them electronically at its banks and so forth, and it prospered. Being a computer of modest habits, it was not given to entertainment and personal consumption of any kind – except for the expenditure of replacing its tax-depreciated hardware, that is to say, part of itself, from time to time. It kept its costs very low. After Dr Frankenstein's death, the Frankenstein Foundation continued to do much good work. The computer made the money, and the Foundation's staff of public-minded (human) employees disbursed the money in accordance with the guidelines laid down by its (human) Board of Directors.

It did not, of course, happen. But if it does not one day happen, it will be more for legal than operational reasons. Perhaps because machines cannot have legal rights and legal liabilities. Or perhaps because machines have no sense of guilt, no good faith and are unpunishable.

We happen to be living in the age of discovery of two types of mind – our own minds and machine minds. We do not know how our own minds work. We are only beginning to discover what part of the brain performs what functions, how, what mechanisms are involved and how self-consciousness is possible. We stand before the mystery of our own minds and know less about them than we know about the 'minds' of computers. There is no good reason to assume that evolution, both natural and artificial, cannot lead to similar results: self-conscious, reasoning beings. Hence one cannot in principle assume that machines will *never* be persons.

Shall we proceed to make such beings? Knowing man, and the

likelihood of very profitable applications, the bet must be on yes. With our usual readiness to taste of the Tree of Knowledge, we shall proceed. No need for us, with great curiosity, to seek extra-terrestrial intelligences in the universe beyond: we are about to fashion them ourselves right here.

Will they be useful? Yes, for many purposes. Self-critical systems are needed in programs whose length has grown so labyrinthine that no programmer can find the faults within it; in programs where the greater error hides the lesser error, and the lesser error hides the greater error; in programs which have to make diagnoses at speeds impossible for man; in conditions, on other planets or in space, that are beyond our physical endurance and our life spans.

However, seeing that such systems would have to possess a value system, and would have to exercise judgements under uncertainty, right or wrong, they would be imperfect machines. They will be beings with their own *eurekas*, and with whatever meaning joy and sorrow may come to have for them.

The last thing needed in business is more imperfect machines; people are enough imperfect machines for this world. Business should stick to perfect cornshellers that never grow any wiser but that grind a thousand or a million bushels serviceably.

Notes

1 E. J. Mishan, 'Fact, Faith & Myth', *Encounter*, Nov. 1986.
2 J. Weizenbaum, *Computer Power and Human Reason*, W. H. Freeman, New York, 1976.

16

Business, Computers and Society

A Symbol of the Age of Information

Computer technology, writes David Bolter, is a 'defining technology'. By this he means a technology that defines man's role in relation to nature.[1]

The spindle – the 'Spindle of Necessity' twisting the thread of life around its whorl – was a symbol for the ancient world. Until the Enlightenment, the clock was a token for the motion of the heavens and the earth's place in it. Later, in the age of steam, great engines symbolized the times. Now the computer is a symbol of the age of information. It is our *ratio cognoscendi*, the way we apprehend the world. It is more: it is the enabling reality which makes excursions of the mind beyond the mind's unaided talents possible.

Unlike some technologies of the past – steam engines, for example – the computer will not be superseded. It will remain with us for as long as our civilization lasts, and for as long as there are businesses to run. It may shrink in size; its underlying technology may move from electronics to photonics; it may continue using binary representation or other forms; but we shall keep its sorting powers. There never were devices before which promised to be a symbiote of man. Beyond a point, increase in quantity leads to a change in quality. This change will happen – is already happening – in the application of computers, but the quality of civilization which may emerge from this is unpredictable.

This is a strange technology indeed – a technology without a Copernicus or a Newton or an Einstein. There are no Nobel Prize winners to be found in this industry.[2] But then neither have any businessmen been honoured by a Nobel Prize for being good businessmen: perhaps because praise and prize, price and piracy, are words that have a common root. Few ordinary people greet the names of Charles Babbage, Alan Turing and John von Neumann with recognition. The thousands of men who developed computers, bit by bit, are anonymous to history. Nobody puts the name of the author of some ingenious software on the label of a floppy disk. Their names, unlike those of writers, composers, or actors, are not to be seen or heard. Computers are a technology of corporations.

A defining technology *re*defines. This technology started by redefining business methods. In 1911, Hermann Hollerith, who used punched-card machines based on the early nineteenth-century Jacquard loom which was designed to make complicated textile patterns, merged his business with others to form the Computing Tabulating Recording Company – later the International Business Machines Corporation. John von Neumann and Norbert Wiener did their best work just after the Second World War on the logic and applications of digital machines.

It has now grown so great in quantity that it redefines the quality of civilization. A cowboy from a small Texas town was aboard a flight from Houston to New York. He had never before left Texas. Starting from a peek at a friend's new personal computer, this man had discovered in himself an unusual talent for programming and program design. A short man with tall boots, a tall hat and string tie, he had become well known and had been hired by a major corporation to recast its information systems. He is now lost to cow-punching, to his own advantage and America's. In this plain man the borders of simplicity and genius had crossed. He was one of many men with talents the world had never needed until now.

Here, then, is an original profession for people who in the past had the wit to play games for amusement – chess, bridge, poker, crossword puzzles – and for an even larger number who might have had the talent to play games, but did not do so because there was no money in them: people without a claim to scholarship, but with a knack for logical procedures. They can now put their talent to well-paid use in an artisanship which is new to the world. The computer has created an entirely new category of superior employment, and man has been promoted.

An Extension of Man

The rewards of invention and social change often benefit a succeeding generation. Those industries which manufacture, service, write for and operate computers employ many people. They also displace many. This has occurred before, and many new technologies have been accused of inhumanity. In 1811, Luddite rioters, seeking revenge, roamed the English countryside to destroy the machines that had displaced them. Also in England, in 1835, a committee of handloom weavers reported that, as a result of the introduction of the power loom, the weekly wages of their members had eroded. Between 1797 and 1804, a man's wage had bought 281 pounds by weight of equal quantities of flour, oatmeal, potatoes and meat. Between 1804 and 1811, 238 pounds. From 1811 to 1818, only 131 pounds – a fall to less than half in about seven years. Yet, while other displacements were more massive, they passed into common habit without outrage. It is not so much change itself, as the rate of change, that makes the difference between acceptance and objection.

The increased productivity of agriculture in the United States in the last hundred years, for example, diverted millions from land to other employment. In 1880, agriculture in the USA employed about eight million people, or approximately 14 per cent of a population of fewer than sixty million people; in 1960, 7 per cent; today, some 2 per cent of a population of about 230 million people, and shrinking.

Similar shifts have taken place in Europe and Japan. Russians today complain that this migration has in great measure ceased in their country and that, consequently, the flow of labour into industry has diminished. In the USSR, about 25 per cent of the population still work the land, more than twelve times as many as in the United States.

In the last hundred years many tens of millions of farmers' children have turned to new skills and found work elsewhere. But one doubts whether any farmer would today wreck his tractors and harvesters in protest, simply because agricultural machines and improved yields have forced some of his children to work, first in Detroit, then in Silicon Valley, for over twenty dollars an hour – plus benefits.

The computer industry is a voracious user of labour. Writing software, for example, is certainly more labour-intensive than any work other than perhaps portrait-painting. The American economist

Lester Thurow points out that the number of accountants in the United States increased from about one million in 1978 to one and one-third million in 1986, in precisely the kind of profession in which computers might have been expected to reduce employment. He points out that in American banks – institutions that have computerized more than almost any other American industry – employment rose by 21 per cent from 1977 to 1982, far outstripping the rise in banking output. Like the wheel, the computer reduces work, in a sense, but also like the wheel, it multiplies its own many uses and adds to work.

Like the wheel, it is ubiquitous and enters into more and more of what we use – subtly redefining and extending almost all our procedures and our tools. Steam and later electricity redefined industry; the power-loom redefined weaving; movable type redefined printing. Computers and micro-processors are less limited and differ: they permeate all manufacturing industries, all service industries and all of daily life alike.

The high rates of unemployment which have affected Western countries because of the fast rate of change from basic to other industries, are matters of profound concern. But what is more disturbing is that we may be arriving at a redefinition of employability and non-employability. It may well be that the computer revolution has something to do with this. An advanced society in the age of computers needs people with a degree of intelligence above the natural level of a sizeable percentile of our species. It is, as yet, too early for conclusions. But if it comes to pass that the basic qualification for membership in societies like ours is scaled too high, and that we are destined to have two nations within the body social – one, numerous, that has more than the minimum requirements for membership, the other, small, having less than the minimum – the future of civic tranquillity is in doubt. Will it do to have two species, one called *homo sapiens*, and another not *sapiens* enough?

Production and Service

Computers blur the distinction between small and large businesses. It is no longer possible to distinguish between the one and the other by counting the numbers employed, or by the amount of capital invested per employee.

A small and peaceful New Jersey town of two thousand inhabitants, one hour's drive from New York, had a road sign which urged 'Caution. Ducks Crossing'. There was, also, in this quiet town, a small company with a very large computer, working day and night. One occasionally saw one person, perhaps two, silhouetted against back-lighted windows late at night. Hundreds of reels of computer tape inside indicated that the company used an enormous data base. It produced and sold direct-mailing lists. Here was a cottage industry redefined. The capital cost, estimated, was between $150,000 and $250,000 per employee, much higher than that of most manufacturing companies. The entire town would, in the past, have been unable to supply the clerical labour to run such mailing lists by hand. Nor would that have been possible: because of proneness to human error, for one; because of cost, for another.

The conclusion to be drawn from what happened there, and is happening everywhere, is that the distinction between small and large business is no longer fully relevant. Small, highly capitalized business has the advantage of proximity to its local market, and will continue to have it. Nor, any longer, is the traditional distinction between production and services always useful. What is common to both is industrialization. If, for example, flexible manufacturing becomes the norm, so that a fully computerized manufacturing line can make specially tailored products for any client at small or no additional cost, then the services of a bespoke tailor and the bespoke products of a manufacturer will have merged into a product/service continuum. Flexible manufacture has other advantages: first, lower inventory needs; then, short but profitable manufacturing runs. Lastly, by being capable of responding flexibly to individual requirements, it reduces the competitiveness of unflexibly mass-produced imports.

Can a clear distinction any longer be made between goods and services? It might be said that services are something one cannot keep in inventory, and that, unlike goods, services cannot be dropped on one's foot. But what is a computer data base if it is not an inventory analogous to physical inventories? Both must be maintained, both are subject to obsolescence, both represent locked-up capital.

This industrialization is happening in manufacturing and in services alike. Industrialization in service companies is industrialization in the same sense as a mechanization of assembly lines. One study estimates that even in industrial corporations, about 'three-quarters of the total value added in the goods sector is created by *service* activities within the sector.'[3] If this is so, then the United States' 1985

Gross National Product of about four trillion dollars consisted on only some three hundred billions, or 7.5 per cent, of tangible manufactured goods.

It is impossible, in practice, to classify services within a manufacturing corporation separately from the manufacturing operations to which they appertain. But if this is admitted, then neither can service sectors be considered apart from manufacturing sectors. If, for example, following the findings mentioned above, General Motors is three-quarters services and one-quarter manufacturing operations, then it is somewhat arbitrary to classify its independent distribution network as wholly a service industry – except in the sense that distributors are financially separate from General Motors. But even then, they are financially separate only if one does not count the importance of the General Motors Acceptance Corporation to these distributors and dealers. In 1985, GMAC, which finances consumer loans for car purchases, had 75 billion dollars in assets, and in that year accounted for over one-quarter of General Motors' entire profits, as also for an unknown additional profit to the dealers.

According to another examination, the capital intensity in the United States, at book value per employee, was about $83,000 in manufacturing, and about $84,000 in all services. But the capital intensity of non-retail services was $139,000, far greater than the *per capita* investment in manufacturing.[4] Seen the other way round, manufacturing uses more labour than non-retail services.

Production and services are a continuum. Where, as in the Soviet Union, the Eastern Bloc and China, production has been the object of official worship, and services not, a discontinuum has become apparent which cannot be simply cured by increasing production there yet more.

It is, however, one of the delusions of our day that manufacturing is in retreat and that the world is becoming increasingly dominated by services. The proposition is false. We have not yet become a post-industrial society; we have not even begun to be one in any real sense. We are, instead, in an age when almost every activity, from making maps to playing games, is a prospect for industrialization.

The total output of manufactured products is still increasing. The appearance of shrinkage is not due to fewer manufactures but to the smaller proportion of people needed to make them. People, not goods, are being deindustrialized in manufacturing, while, at the same time, people are being industrialized in service industries.

It is true that modern materials and technology make it possible to achieve more with a lesser weight of raw materials and at lesser cost. But this is irrelevant to the general argument: artifacts are made in ever greater numbers to meet an unceasing world demand. With great economy, electrical transmission, for example, uses less copper and less sheathing; optical cabling increases the volume of transmitted signals beyond all proportion to the amount of material in the conduit; small satellites take the place of thousands of miles of wire. Compared with the heavy radio receivers using thermionic values, modern transistorized receivers are small and light, but there are millions more of the latter than there ever were of the former.

Efficiency has increased: Switzerland, in 1979–80, used 371 kilograms of coal (or its energy equivalent) to produce $1,000 of gross domestic product, while the USSR still used 1,490 kilograms to achieve the same purpose. Switzerland used 26 kilograms of steel, while the USSR used 135, to produce the same addition to its gross domestic product. The comparison does not flatter the USSR – even though the Soviets produce far more energy and far more steel than the Swiss.[5]

To the second proposition – that the world will be increasingly dominated by services – there are two objections. The first is that the apparent growth of services is as much a result of the increasing productivity of the manufacturing sector as it is the result of the growth of new services. If industry needs fewer people, there *must* be a statistical shift into either services or else unemployment.

The other reply to the shift-to-services argument is that services are, and will continue to be, of much lesser importance in world trade than manufactured and other tangible goods. In the USA, services now represent 71 per cent of the gross national product, and 75 per cent of all jobs. These proportions are similar in other Western economies. But in world trade, measurable services account for only about 30 per cent of the total. This component of world trade (with the exception, perhaps, of licensing and similar invisibles) is unlikely to grow to more than about a third of total trade, since services like surgery and supermarkets, firemen and funerals, street-cleaning and schools, and other things of that genus, are scarcely promising subjects for world trade. Raw materials, minerals and food,[6] which were about one-third and are now about one-fifth, and manufactures, which are about one-half of world trade, will keep their preponderance.

But even as the distinction between manufacturing and services wanes, one distinction remains of which we must remind ourselves: the distinction between jobs that make men sweat and jobs that don't. And we might also remind ourselves that, ultimately, *all* business is a service industry.

Notes

1. David Bolter, *Turing's Man*, University of North Carolina, Chapel Hill, N.C., 1984.
2. The discoverers of the transistor-effect were awarded a Nobel Prize in 1956. Nothing since.
3. *United States National Study on Trade in Services*, Office of the US Trade Representative, Washington DC, Dec. 1983.
4. J. B. Quinn and C. E. Gagnon, 'Will Services follow Manufacturing into Decline?' *Harvard Business Review*, Nov/Dec 1986. The retail sector, with its lower investment of only $38,000 per capita, makes the average capital intensity in industry and services similar.
5. *Economist*, London, 6 July 1985.
6. These have diminished as a proportion of world trade because the price of oil has fallen, and the terms of trade have been unfavourable to producers of food and staples.

    It is often believed that the service component in international trade is growing fast. As GATT figures make clear, it is the international trade in manufactures which has risen faster than measurable services:

World Trade, excluding Eastern Bloc, in billions of dollars

	1981	1987	Increase (%)
Total	2,591	3,210	23.9
of which:			
Manufactures	1,044	1,643	57.4
Services	771	959	24.4
Agriculture	274	312	13.9
Mining & oil	502	296	−41.0 (decrease)

Section 7

Business in Society

Preamble

Civilization is not precise: one can only survey its hazy landscapes and constituent parts, its plains and mountains, rivers and forests – and say that 'civilization lies about here.'[1]

Earlier cultures did not consider change, and the idea of change, to be ideal ingredients of civility. Most of them were devoted to a given order of things and were not kind to those who tried to subvert that order – including merchants. But Western civilization, whose carriers are science, technology and business, differs. In a technological business-civilization the process of change is fundamental. Rightly or wrongly, change is seen as a hub of progress.

There are other hubs: creativity and continuity; fellowship; refinement; humanity, tolerance and balance; equality and rank; and honesty. One may then ask which of these, or their absence, shape and are shaped by business.

We begin with creativity and continuity.

By itself, a civilization is not necessarily creative. It is only (as was once said by an orchestral conductor) absolutely superb at producing second violins.

In 1928, an elegant book on civilization claimed that the essential characteristic of a highly civilized society is not that it is creative, but that it is appreciative. 'Savages create furiously,' it said.[2] But they do not. Savages *live* furiously; they create little; they are frantically busy just surviving. That is why, perhaps, the history of early man was so long and his own life so short.

Another writer, Sombart, held the view that culture, being an estrangement from nature, carries in itself the germs of dissolution, destruction and death. But it does not. A businessman's answer is that culture, being part of human nature, carries in itself the germs of evolution, creation and life. Business is by its nature inclined to creation and optimism. (If it is sometimes also professionally wary and full of caution it is only because for specific purposes pessimists are often better informed.) Business cannot be resigned, defeatist or despairing. It is not possible to run a business and make a profit that way.

One way to try to sustain a civilization is to sanctify unchangingness. Another way to preserve it is by continuous change, improvement and evolution. This other way came to us through the Enlightenment and after. It was the way of the planets of enterprise around the fixed sun of the American Constitution, and it still is the way of business. Despite its many failures and retreats, fundamental hopefulness is characteristic of business. Arguably, science and technology, with business as their commissioner and disseminator, are still the chief reasons for faith in the buoyancy of (at least) material progress. New discoveries compel science to change its concepts, and competition does the same for business. Whatever the case, the idea that continuous change can provide continuity to a civilization is new.

As to fellowship:

Man may be a social animal but he is not a very social animal. While it is true that savages are always to be found in each others' company, that is because they have no alternative. Civilized man, on the contrary, is as much a solitary and private animal as he is a social animal. True, he spends a great deal of money on companionship and much of his time with friends and colleagues. But he spends far more money on privacy. He may not even be fond of his fellow men: it is said of the English that they do not like each other but trust no one else; and of Americans, that they like and trust each other but not with money.

Privacy is of special concern to civilization. Companionship is often expensive but privacy is always expensive. Since industry and business create the wealth which pays for the luxury of privacy, we may justifiably maintain that if privacy has any value, it is a value sustained by the industriousness of business. There is, of course, no relationship of intimacy between business and privacy, but there is certainly a relationship of intimate dependence between them.

As to refinement:

Good taste may adorn a civilization, but may also stifle it. The thin-blooded Heian aristocracy of Japan, mentioned elsewhere in these pages, was an example. In another case, the exquisite nobility of the *ancien régime* of France, haughty in every rank, was divided into three: the Nobility of the Sword, the even more exquisite Nobility of Breeding and the judicial Nobility of the Robe. Had it not been for a continuous elevation of new nobles to the Robe, and the flushing of its noble ranks by waves of newly raised and patented merchants, bankers and other worthies, French aristocracy would have been almost completely without merit. Aristocrats of good taste but great sterility would probably have been impaled on the pitchforks of the peasantry long before they were carted away on the tumbrils of the Revolution.

A civilization must not be entirely pure; it must have gaps of taste. There should be room in it for cheerful plainness and lively vulgarity. If it is too tightly swaddled in delicate refinement, it loses its refreshment. It is an equivocal compliment to commerce to say that it has always been able to inject earthiness into civilization. But the compliment is deserved in its good, as well as in the other sense.

It is in any case not necessary to argue that businessmen are civilized. Some are and some are not: needless to say, many are intolerant, irrational, lawless, unstable and unreliable. Don't trust these tellers – but don't despair of the tale; not the civility of individual businessmen, but their aggregate effect, is what matters to a civilization.

There is a reservation: in 1988, a Japanese insurance company bought a Van Gogh flower painting for several tens of millions of dollars. To have one painting hanging by one nail in one office is not civilization. In a civilization, good objects must have good neighbours.

Mercantile taste has had profound effects on the arts. The patronage of seventeenth-century Dutch merchants, for example, changed the art of painting there. No longer was the painter confined to idealized pictures of kings and heroes, or to idealized pictures of sacred virgins, or to the idealized 'triumphs' of both. He now painted Holland's earthy subjects in mellow and unearthly light – paintings of people weighing, counting, measuring, drinking, talking and spinning yarn near kitchens.

Business has not been unkind to the arts, because it traded in luxuries, itself liked luxury and because the arts were its relaxation.

As to humanity, tolerance, and balance:

The classical age considered man to be the measure of all things. In business, the market is that measure. Which is all right as far as it goes, but leaves one a little uneasy because the market has no market for humanity and tolerance. There is, to be sure, a safeguard: one cannot choose customers for their (or one's own) private inclinations and beliefs. One can only choose them for their buying power, and one must, therefore, have regard for them.

However doubtful its own concern for tolerance, business has stolidly borne the intolerance of others through the ages. Ulysses, returning from many hardships to his native Ithaca, was taunted for being a merchant who only cared for 'the gains of his greed'. And the gentleman of ancient Greece, the handsome and shining *kalos kagathos*, while he should have the means to enjoy the 'exquisite delight' of leisure, was not to engage in trade and in the crafts. Like many Romans, Cicero found tax-collecting and moneylending too low for gentlemen: 'these occupations arouse enmity.' Keeping shop, even a perfume shop, was vulgar. Big business was (barely) acceptable but the most becoming occupation for a gentleman was agriculture. In the age of feudal precedence, traders suffering pain were more common than traders inflicting it. If they were poor enough, they had to sell their wares from door to door, or on the street corners of first one town and then another. Wretched men – Christians, Jews, even Muslims – plodded the roads of Europe, peddling their wares. Itinerant merchant-salesman (and there were at first few others), in the England of the eleventh and twelfth centuries, were called piepowders (or *pieds poudreux*, dusty-footed men – literally, because paved roads had not been built since Roman days). Even in the seventeenth century, John Locke, a rational man, regarded trade as 'wholly inconsistent with a gentleman's calling'.

The idea of tolerance is not old. It arose in the sixteenth and seventeenth centuries as a result of religious indifference (Michel de Montaigne, the essayist) or of religious principles (William Penn, the Quaker) or of dispassionate logic (Pierre Bayle, the author of philosophical dictionaries) or of the French Catholic *politiques* who argued for the toleration of Protestants.[3]

To balance the view, two examples of intolerant business: slave-trding and piracy. Venice in the ninth century, though it used few slaves, dealt in many. The sale of eunuchs 'Made in Venice' to Eastern courts was particularly lucrative. The Church was no hindrance to the trade; she tolerated the enslavement of pagans and infidels. She reasoned – oh, for the flexibility of conscience – that the bondage of their persons might lead to the salvation of their souls.

Not until well after the French Revolution, and within the living memory of the children of liberated American slaves, did the practice of slavery cease. It ceased, as Thomas Carlyle remarked, because one half of all Americans preferred to hire their servants for life and the other half preferred to hire them by the hour. It was recently reported that Angolan women had been shipped to Cuba for work in conditions of serfdom, in exchange for Cuban soldiery to Angola. Fortunately for the reputation of business, neither Angola nor Cuba need necessarily be viewed as vigorous defenders of the market system.

Commerce often began with piracy. Having to sell the goods they had stolen changed pirates into traders. Before the ninth century, Swedish Vikings began to raid the land of the Slavs. They sought amber and furs, honey and slaves – males for labour, females for Eastern harems. They were Varangian Vikings who called themselves the Rus. In about the ninth century, the Vikings established trading posts from the Baltic to the Black Sea to serve as collection points and in due course turned more trader than raider. In this way it came about, approximately, that the Slavs (whose name in their own tongue means 'fame', 'glory' or 'repute') gave us the word slave, and that their predators, the Rus, gave us the name of Russia. The Russians continued to be enslaved throughout the reigns of the Rurikid succession which included Ivan the Terrible and that of the Romanovs which included Peter the Great and Catherine the Great, until, in 1861, serfdom was remitted by Czar Alexander the Second, only to be resumed by Hitler and Stalin, the Mad and the Cruel respectively. Most of those mentioned are a part of the political opposition that Gorbachev now faces.

As to equality and rank:

Business does not aim at equality. It aims at inequality and advantage. It aims at gain even when it means another's loss. It aims at victory over competitors – competitors who are not enemies but not friends either. The businessman will go where the profits are and take up a trade which may destroy them. He may thus be seen to be a cause of inequality. But it is not that simple.

Paradoxically, an excess of equality tends to favour inequality. If talent is not allowed to rise to the top, there must be someone to stop it from ascending. Titled and untitled commissars are found to push rising heads under water. To keep commoners in their proper place and station, a class of superiors exists to keep them 'equal'.

Whether or not it accords with a strict view of evenhanded justice and equality, effort deserves a higher than average reward; it is the better justice. All this is not to say that inequality of reward and equality before the law cannot coexist, but it is to say that philosophies of social justice must be taken with a pinch of salt, because, when complete equality becomes an irresistible force, complete justice immediately becomes an immovable object.

Business has, nevertheless, been a source of social equality. Not because it creates equality – it does not – but because entry is reasonably open. Vacancies always occur. With every new generation and every change of circumstance, new doors open to eager entrants. An acceptance of free commerce, and even freer arts, must either be one of the values of a civilization, or else, at the price of stagnation, their enemy.

Lastly, a peculiar and often fatal form of colour blindness among successful businessmen was, historically, their preference for blue blood over red.

Dukes, we know, are attracted to large expanses of dirt as their enduring source of wealth and standing. But the Dutch, in the seventeenth century, and other nations later, proved that there are more sources of enduring stability and wealth than land. At the same time, Blaise Pascal noted that the sober and sensible Swiss began to take offence if you called them gentlemen; to be considered worthy of high office, they had to show the common and plebeian touch.

The pursuit of rank is a vestige of history. Feudalism has died, and so, without leaving a worthwhile legacy, has absolute and heroic monarchy. In retrospect, heroic kingship proved to have been mostly heel and almost no Achilles. Elevation to high and noble rank has not been good for business: an elevated commoner was expected to cease from the visible pursuit of commercial gain, which, when he did, destroyed his business and his wealth in one or two succeeding generations.

As to honesty:

The Greek ideal of *arete*, of noble excellence, while it had something to do with beauty, had little to do with morality. The rough ethics of medieval knights and nobles have been mentioned. It has also been noted that kings found reasons of state more persuasive than reasons of conscience. The Church, too, was hard on men like Galileo and Darwin, who were not only careful observers of nature, but honest. Galileo's greater and Darwin's older world by magnifying God diminished man – an inconvenient truth.

We have also observed, by contrast, the development of maritime law by merchants at a time when Europe was landlocked, and when its medieval kings concerned themselves with territorial laws and rules of war on dry land. Merchants devised a *jus mercatorum* or commercial code to settle disputes and regulate commercial customs, and means of exchange to lubricate international trade. Business replaced the concept of knightly honour with the practice of honesty. Merchants made their own civility. Since these jurisdictions had little standing in official courts of law, they had recourse to arbitrators chosen from amongst their own ranks. They were outside the feudal order; they often did what the church forbade. They brought into the currency of daily life the rationale of money, the practical meaning of interest on loans, the morality of equitable sharing, the modes of cooperative venture in various forms, the tit for tat, the give and take, the settlement of debt, the granting of credit on trust, the avoidance (generally) of war in the face of conflict. The principle that *pacta sunt servanda*, bargains are to be kept, was a step forward not only for business, but for all civilized human intercourse. Unlike some kings and governments, they held to civilized 'standards below which things must not fall'. And even though it was all done for the sake of profit, when done well there was some good in it.

The preconditions for a private enterprise system, says one informed writer,[4] include a well-designed system of property rights; acceptable standards of weights and measures; ready access to courts of law; the enforceability of contracts; effective protection for life and property; dependence on mutual trust; and personal rectitude. Should these erode, he says, the market system would become increasingly expensive and inefficient and ultimately inoperable.

Honesty in business is less a moral sentiment than a part of self-interest. Businessmen are buffeted by circumstance and must make their own accommodation with conscience. But at least most would agree with Abraham Lincoln that one should choose another occupation, 'rather than one in the choosing of which one does, in advance, consent to be a knave'.

Notes

1 Clive Bell, *Civilization*, Chatto & Windus, London, 1928, p. 71.
2 ibid.

3 F. L. Nussbaum, *Economic Institutions of Modern Europe*, F. S. Crofts & Co., New York, 1933.
4 E. J. Mishan, 'Fact, Faith & Myth', *Encounter*, Nov. 1986.

17

Business and Civilization

Culture and Government

Even in this century, J. M. Keynes could with justice observe that many practical men hear ancient voices in the air from which they distil their frenzies. They are often 'slaves of some defunct economist' or other shaman.

We have not lived long in ages of reason. For many peoples, reality is still in part the legends with which they veil the sober world. For much of the time mankind has dreamed its way through history. It has been either sustained, or destroyed, by overlays of preconceptions. Man is a myth-maker. His cultural compulsions and superstitions, his gods and his devils, dominate his understanding of events.

In particular, he has held to two persistent and damaging myths. The first was the categorization of society into rigid classes – from the coronation of 'divine' kings and the crowning of chief proletarians, through the ranks of the variously privileged, down to the 'shamefaced poor'. The second is the false interpretations of individual and national self-interest of which this chapter speaks.

History dwells in us long after its events have departed from our lives. Peter Levi, a contemporary, a Jesuit priest for twenty-eight years, recounts that as late as the 1960s, Catholic priests had to swear the Antimodernist Oath before their ordination, which bound them among other details to reject socialism. In his own lifetime, even, the Roman liturgy for Holy Week still contained a prayer for the Holy Roman Emperor – a title which lost its meaning with the death of Charlemagne more than a thousand years ago.[1]

History moves along its single track and it is vain to speculate what might have happened had it moved on another. It didn't and the debate must end. Adam Smith, writing in 1776, agreed and said that to propose that Great Britain should voluntarily give up all authority over her American colonies and leave them to elect their own magistrates, enact their own laws and make peace and war as they might think proper, 'would be to propose such a measure as never was, and never will be adopted, by any nation in the world'.

But what if it had been adopted? If it had, he says, and if Great Britain had settled with the Americans such a treaty of commerce as would secure to Americans a free trade more advantageous to her people than the monopoly Britain at the time enjoyed, and if, thus, they had parted good friends, then 'the natural affection of the colonies to the mother country, which, perhaps, our late dissensions have well nigh extinguished, would quickly revive.' Then, Smith added, instead of being turbulent and factious subjects, they might become faithful, affectionate and generous allies. Smith went on to suggest that Americans should be represented in the British Parliament in substantial numbers from the very beginning, in proportion to the taxes they contributed. America's progress in wealth, population and improvement, he said, had been so rapid that in the course of little more than a century, perhaps, America's tax contribution might exceed Britain's. 'The seat of the empire would then naturally remove itself to that part of the empire which contributed most to the general defence and support of the whole' – which is to say from Britain to America.

One cannot be entirely convinced that Smith's recommendations have lost much of their good sense in the more than two centuries since they were propounded. But, 'such a measure never was, and never will be adopted, by any nation in the world.' Nations rarely jump the hurdles of their preconceptions.

In the event, what happened? The Founders of the American Republic knew that they confronted greatness and great danger: not from Britain, but danger that some caesar might arise; that the ascent of America might be subject to corrosion by rapacity and moral decay; that the virtues of republicans might become the evils of a mob; that the democratic electorate was as likely to be incontinent as decent; and that America's could as probably be a destiny of failure as of greatness. There was 'a darker strain in the thoughts of the Founders'. They believed in progress, but knew that republics 'lived and died by virtue – and that in the fullness of time power and luxury inexorably brought corruption and decay'.[2]

The strength of Americans, whether in business or in foreign policy, in social experimentation or in domestic policy, was their awareness that America is – as it was at its beginnings and continues to be – an experiment, a domestic but undomesticated chiliastic experiment. Americans believed themselves to be their own saviours, and they tested every law and every liberty to its ultimate limits. They continue to test it; the experiment runs on. The founding of the United States was an experiment in nationhood, but it was an experiment in civility as well. The Union was 'the first historical attempt to give back to the individual what the State had stolen from the person in the beginning'.[3]

In both Europe and the United States, political power dominates. But more than in the countries of Western Europe, American industrial and business civilization envelops the life of the nation, leaving culture outdistanced though strongly in the race. A balance between the three elements – culture, government, business – will only be reached in the third century of the existence of the Republic. In the meantime, the United States, while accused of its materialism, is admired for its spirit.

In time, power inexorably brought corruptions. But it brought only one form of decay: a conviction that America was naturally destined for greatness and that her destiny was cheerfully manifest. This kind of national conceit reduced another nation, Britain, from unchallengeable heights to average significance.

Britain's civility has hardened but not vanished. She still has many and decent values – too many perhaps. But clear judgement on the *purpose* of work is no longer one of them. She understands money in a particular way, but her views on the nexus between money and work – that deep affinity – are sometimes muddled. Puritanism, except for pockets of it here and there, has vanished from the British scene, and has as yet not been replaced by an enlightened and expansive materialism. Her illusion is that her present mirrors her past. Unfortunately (probably in Acton's words), the devil changed the content of her bottles without altering their labels.

The evidence for conceit is old. In 1732, Daniel Defoe was able to say 'without the least partiality to our own country', that 'i. We are not only a trading country, but the greatest trading country in the world. ii. Our climate is the most agreeable climate in the world to live in. [A sentiment on which umbrella-makers may cast some doubt.] iii. Our Englishmen are the stoutest and best [crafts]men . . . in the world.'[4]

Some one hundred years later, a committee of the House of Commons voiced the view that

> although Europe were possessed of every tool now used in the United Kingdom . . . yet, from the natural and acquired advantages possessed by this country, the manufacturers of the United Kingdom would for ages continue to retain the superiority they now enjoy. The many important facilities . . . which we possess, are enjoyed by no other country; nor is it likely that any country can enjoy them to an equal extent for an indefinite period. Our skill is unrivalled; the industry and power of our people unequalled; their ingenuity . . . without parallel; and apparently, without limit.[5]

Two incongruities divide Britain. The first is that it is, in one respect, a society of deep roots, in another, a society that lives by its wits. Britain has deeply rooted institutions: parliament, freedoms, laws, as well as habits. But in matters of business, with some exceptions, it is not a society that lives by a corpus of inherited commitments. No deep-rooted managerial tradition exists. Management is each new manager's adventure.

The other incongruity was noticed by Ralph Waldo Emerson: on the one hand 'an Englishman shows no mercy to those below him in the social scale, as he looks for none from those above him.' On the other hand 'the English have given importance to individuals, a principal end and fruit of every society.'[6] As Emerson noticed in his day, and despite the incongruity, this respect for the principles of individual justice made it possible for the English, in addition to their own law, to administer broadmindedly the codes of every race; in Canada, old French law; in Mauritius, the Code Napoleon; in the West Indies, the edicts of the Spanish Cortes; in the East Indies, the laws of Menu; in the Isle of Man, the Scandinavian 'Thing'; at the Cape of Good Hope, of the old Netherlands; and in the Ionian Islands, the Pandects of Justinian.

And, therefore, civility is not one of Britain's problems. Her problem is that her civility has not yet found a comfortable place for business.

Exchange and Natural Instinct

To see where the businessman stands amid his civilization, we recall the image of its past ideal members. There was the *kalos kagathos*, the balanced and luminous man of ancient Greece; the Roman gentleman of dignity and *gravitas*; the English gentleman; the *honnête homme* and *gentilhomme* of France, and earlier, her *preux chevalier* or gallant knight.

We shall instantly be struck by the fact that the sweat of labour was not part of their image. We may also notice that, while they were the ideal children of their civilization, they did not always furnish its leadership. They were indispensable symbols of their civilization but lived to little other purpose. They had magnificent form but form without any significant economic function.

With the coming of the businessman, something was added to the image and something to the reality. An eighteenth- and nineteenth-century English and American gentleman could not be counted a gentleman *unless he had something to do*. He earned respect by his function and it was his function that gave him his form.

He also had a second consolation denied to many other occupations. Whereas poetry is mute in a society which appreciates only prose, and whereas scholarship is useless amid barbarism, the businessman could always remember that Adam was his own Tailor, and award himself the distinction of wealth – useful at any time and anywhere.

But, beyond wealth, the magnet of elitism still attracts the businessman. If he is rich enough in Britain, he sends his sons to private schools (there known as public schools) to acquire the habits of accomplished *sprezzatura* – of 'high-caste gallantry' and easy, throw-away grace. In France it is his ambition to see his son – less so his daughter – attend a *grande école*. There the son will make good friends who will promote him or whom he will promote later in life. Salem (or similar schools) may do the same for German fathers.

In the United States of America, the successful businessman was, as Oliver Wendell Holmes said in the middle of the nineteenth century, 'forming an aristocracy . . . very splendid, though its origins may have been tar, tallow, and train-oil'.[7] His sons, Holmes concluded, need not win their spurs, but must at least gild them. Fortunately for America, ordinary people, who were themselves busily digging for gold, were blind to gilt. Exclusiveness in America remained an indoor sport for Boston Brahmins and their hangers-on, who may not have remembered that only kings are crowned by their inferiors – and there was little chance of that in the United States.

It is as well that Americans did not accept the claims of elites, because elites find democracy indigestible. Business is not equipped to be a permanent elite. For one thing, leadership cannot be passed from one generation to the next for long. For another, leadership is (as indeed it should be) based on talent and is not necessarily joined to ownership. Lastly, the case may be made – though it cannot be proved – that the populism of American business inhibited business elites in Europe from trying to become permanent. The worst aspect of elites, who otherwise are only clubs and cannot do much harm, is their inclination to want to become hereditary.

Civilization is generally concerned with qualities and values. But civilization does not put a firm price on its values. To Western civilization, business added the rationale of rigorous economic calculus and price. One may agree that the new criteria of business – cheap and dear – were not the same as the criteria of good and bad. One may also agree that cheaper and dearer are rarely the same as better and worse. But in the event, price comparisons proved to be more amenable and less contestable than moral, aesthetic and qualitative comparisons. One knew where one stood with price, but values fluctuated and floundered. It was, therefore, not surprising that the calculi of commerce won in the making of our present civilization.

Now, it can be argued that the criterion of price is materialistic; that it is less than human; that it is spiritless and crude. To this one may firstly reply that there was not much spirituality in the empires of Alexander the Great, in Rome, in the Mogul conquest of China or in the Russian Revolution either – in none of which power was in the least commercial. One may next say that art was often more abundant and inspired in materialistic civilizations like those of Florence, Venice and the Netherlands Republic than in 'spiritual' civilizations like biblical Palestine or present-day Iran. One may lastly consider the word materialism and point out that it is much abused.

Dictionaries will define materialism as the tendency to prefer material possessions and physical comfort to spiritual values. But is it the joy of material possession alone, or another kind of joy, to receive a Christmas gift from one's family and friends or to take pleasure at the acquisition of a painting? And is it a pure materialism of physical comfort to take a hot shower after dusty work? And was it indeed spirituality for the medieval church to justify the enslavement of barbarians on the grounds that the bondage of their persons would lead to the salvation of their souls? Was it simply materialism when merchants chose to trust one another's promises to pay instead of threatening each other with brandished swords like knights – even though these promises were made for bolts of damask and bundles of spice? Materialism is not the love of money, objects, comfort. Materialism is the love of these alone, and of nothing else by rich men, not by the huddled poor. And to repeat, it is not necessary to argue that because many individual businessmen are 'materialistic', some materialism is morally bad in general.

More than to love money and what it will buy, materialism is to believe that things are as they are, to be satisfied with what is, to be smug, to rest on equilibrium, to plead that present virtues are sufficient and that present vices are convenient.

Exchange is not a natural instinct. The natural instinct of mankind is to wrest the fruits of every 'poor inch of nature'. It is to take – and take without requitement or reciprocity. Nor is man naturally inclined to wait and defer satisfactions. The idea of equitable exchange and the idea of deliberate deferment of satisfaction are civilized ideas. The first step was the change from the impatience of the hunter to the patience of the peasant who waits for months between sowing and reaping.

What business has added to the calculi of civilization is, as we have seen, the price and the profit of waiting – waiting for the interest on a loan, for the return on an investment, and waiting until the cost of initial effort becomes income later.

The businessman has never abandoned, and never will abandon, the keen and restless eye of the pirate. His methods have changed, his buccaneering instincts have remained. He has never been very selective *whom* he served. He has served honest and dishonest men. He has served kings and leaders of high and low morality. He has not greatly cared *what* he sold. He sold arms to kill, food to eat, clothes to keep one warm, valuable jewels, and baubles to deceive the eye. But he had always to be careful *how* he served and could never ignore his obligations.

There is no need for him to tread the 'austere road of virtue', or break his neck from the perpetual exercise of turning the other cheek. A little less than that will do quite well. He will never achieve the ideal of civilization. But he will not even get near it without standards.

Notes

1. *The Frontiers of Paradise: a Study of Monks and Monasteries*, Collins Harvill, London, 1987, pp. 72 and 91.
2. Arthur M. Schlesinger Jr. *The Cycles of American History*, Andre Deutsch, London, 1987.
3. Octavio Paz, *One Earth, Four or Five Worlds*, Harcourt Brace Jovanovich, New York, 1985.
4. Daniel Defoe, *The Complete English Tradesman*, 3rd edn. 1732, p. 304.
5. Quoted by Charles Babbage in *On the Economy of Machines and Manufactures*, 2nd edn. London, 1832, from a report to the House of Commons 'On the Export of Tools and Machinery'.
6. Ralph Waldo Emerson, 'English Traits', 1847–8.
7. Oliver Wendell Holmes, *The Autocrat of the Breakfast Table*, 1858.

The extracts from Adam Smith are from his *Wealth of Nations*, volume 2, book IV, ch. vii, part III.

Epilogue

We have traced some continuities and discontinuites in the growth of Western business between the twin rocks of spiritual and temporal power; how it has manifested itself in two other cultures; what attributes it has; where it stands in relation to ideology; what propels it now; and what characteristics of civilization it shares.

Last questions remain. Is business perhaps an enemy of civilization? Is its acquisitiveness contemptible? Is its continued expansion a danger to the world? Is its financial power likely to overwhelm hopes of a lively but gentle life? Are its values divorced from, perhaps in opposition to, other, uncommercial values of mankind? Is capitalism an unworthy system to take us into the future?

Had these questions been asked 150 years ago, the answers might have been yes. They *were* then asked by Karl Marx and other, milder socialists. Their answer was an angry yes. If their answer today is more qualified, more subdued, even more humble, what has wrought the change?

The change of outlook came, perhaps, from the realization that capitalism is not a separate and coherent system, nor a coherent ideology. Capitalism is, as we have earlier noted, a critical procedure. It is a procedure in the very simple sense that if someone has an entrepreneurial idea and finds the means for it, he may proceed. It is critical in the equally simple sense that if he does not succeed, he is soon forced to strike camp, and if he does succeed, the continuous critique of competition keeps him on a path.

The life of nations is, of course, shaped in certain distinctive ways by the results of this critical procedure called capitalism. But it is not the only thing that shapes them. If they were uniformly moulded by the playing-out of some universal economic laws, there could be no explanation why distinctive forms of civility and outlook continue –

even increase – in different variants of capitalism: American, British, French, German, Italian, Scandinavian, Japanese. Business civilizations may tend to converge with each other, but, opposing this, history and the wealth of nations tend not only to maintain but to increase diversity and variability. Marx's presumption that there are great laws to move the world 'with iron necessity towards an inexorable destination' was wrong. Such laws do not exist. The rules of business intercourse create a certain unity, but it is a unity amid many continuing diversities.

Capitalism, though distinctive both in kind and contribution, cannot by itself create a new civilization, but it can support and be part of general civility. Business can only survive in an ocean of culture wider and richer than itself. Even the merchant cultures of some Italian cities, of the Netherlands and Germany did not survive more than a century or two. Nor will our Western world survive unharmed if it imagines that business can, by itself alone, carry it into a future both amenable and prosperous.

We now answer our questions. Business is a friend of civilization – if it does not seek to create its own. Acquisitiveness is not contemptible – if it is rational and serves the general purpose. The continued expansion of business is no danger to the world – if it is part of the expansion of a valuable world. Its financial power is not likely to overwhelm hopes of a lively and gentle life – if it is itself hopeful of such a life. Its values are not divorced from, or in opposition to, other, uncommercial values of mankind – if it forswears an arrogance of power.

Index

accelerated information, 160
accountability *see* freedom and accountability
accounting practices, 71–2
achievement, 9
acquisitiveness, 192
　materialism, 185, 188–9
Acton, Lord, 43, 89
Adenauer, Konrad, 13, 57
adventurers *see* mercantilists and adventurers
Alexander, Ivan, ix–xv
Alexander II, 179
Alidosi, 84
ambition, 10–11
Ambrose, St, 73, 101
Amsterdam, 77–8
Amsterdam Insurance Company, 81–2
analytical engine, 153
ancien régime, 176–7
Antimodernist Oath, 183
Antoninus, St, 102, 103
arete, 180
'aristocratic' leaders, 13
aristocracy, 123, 127, 128
　Japan, 134–6
Aristotle, 41, 96
artificial intelligence, 162
arts, 177
asceticism, 113, 114
Augustine, St, 41
Austrian Edict of Toleration, 125
autonomy, entrepreneurship and, 9–12

Babbage, Charles, 153–4, 163, 168
Bacon, Francis, 15, 26, 104, 112, 161
balance of trade (Japan), 143
Bank of England, 115
Barbour, Violet, 78
Barnato, Barney, 23
barratto transaction, 100
Bayle, Pierre, 178
Beard, Miriam, 14–15, 84, 130

being, computers and, 162–5
Berle, Adolf, 60
Bernardino, St, 101
Bernardino of Feltre, 103
bills of exchange, 108, 109
Bismarck, Prince Otto von, 57, 86
Bolter, David, 167
Braudel, Fernand, 76, 98
Bretton Woods agreement, 109
Bridges, Robert, 71
Britain, 185–6
brotherhood, 85, 98–101, 102
Bukharin, N. I., 51
Bullinger, 112
bullion, export of, 108
bureaucracy, 37–8, 83, 86
Burke, Edmund, 57
business
　computers and *see* computers (and business); computers (and society)
　cultures that shaped *see* cultures (that shaped business)
　future of, 51–3
　ideas that shaped *see* ideas (that shaped business)
　information age *see* information age
　movements that shaped *see* movements (that shaped business)
　outsiders, 121–3
　rationale, 89–90
business (attributes of)
　marketing attributes, 23–32
　personal attributes, 9–18
　preamble, 5–7
　taxation attributes, 33–40
　value attributes, 19–21
business and politics *see* politics and business; politics around business; politics in business
business in society
　civilization, 183–9

business in society (*cont.*):
  preamble, 175–81
'buy-and-lease-back' system, 84

Cahorsins, 125
Caligula, 122
Calvin, John, 92, 110–11, 112, 113
Calvinism, 79, 112–13, 114, 132
capital intensity, 172
capitalism, 142, 191–2
  age of steam, 83–5
  business outsiders, 121–3
  early, 83
  free enterprise, 112–16
  merchant class (emergence), 104–6
  politics and, 48–9
  rational speculation, 94–5
capitalism and enterprise
  free enterprise, 112–16
  Reformation and Protestant ethic, 109–12
  transnationalism of money, 107–9
caput, 37
Carlyle, Thomas, 178
Catherine the Great, 179
Catholics, 111, 112, 115
Charlemagne, 73, 97, 183
Charles III, 82
Chesterton, G. K., 56
Christianity and enterprise
  merchant class (emergence), 104–6
  rational speculation, 94–5
  rationality (missing links), 97–103, 107–9
  usury, 95–7
  work, 91–4
Church, 75, 89–90, 180
  money and, 107, 108–12
Churchill, Winston, 13–14, 57
Cicero, 178
cities, 77, 78
civil servants
  excess of in France, 83
  Japan, 140, 145
civility in business enterprise
  civility, 139–42
  Japan, 127–8
  manners, 137–9
  Westering of Japan, 127–8
civilization, business and, 175
  culture and government, 183–6
  epilogue, 191–2
  exchange and natural instinct, 186–9
class consciousness, 85, 86
clustered culture (Japan)
  feudalist origins, 127–9
  Industrial Revolution, 129–30
  mind of Japan, 131–3
  status, 134–6

Cocteau, Jean, 45
coinage, 63–4, 82, 97
Colbert, Jean-Baptiste, 83
colonialism, 20, 76–7, 81, 86, 184
Columbus, Christopher, 81
commerce, 64–6
commercial code, 180
communism, 49–51
compensation, 102
competition, 17, 21, 123–6, 144
computers (and business), 149, 153
  being (and reasoning), 162–5
  early user's introduction, 154–5
  eternity and, 155–7
  information and, 157–9
  knowledge and, 159–62
computers (and society)
  extension of man, 169–70
  information age symbol, 167–8
  production and service, 170–4
Computing Tabulating Recording Company, 168
conceit, 10–11
concessions (in negotiation), 30, 32
confidence, 17
Conrad, Joseph, 115
conservation, politics and, 56–7
conservatism, 56–7
consideration, 63
continuity, 175–6
'country pay', 64
craft production, 66–7
creativity, 175–6
credit, 63, 64, 65, 66, 89
culture, 176
  government and, 183–6
cultures (that shaped business)
  civility in business enterprise, 137–46
  clustered (Japanese), 127–36
  dispersed (Jews), 121–6
  preamble, 119–20

damages (repayment), 100
Darrell, William (Wild), 71
Darwin, Charles, 14, 180
De Beers Consolidated Mines, 23
decision-making, judgement and, 16–18
'defining technology', 167, 168
Defoe, Daniel, 11, 185
de Gaulle, Charles, 13, 57–8
deindustrialization, 172
democracy, taxation in, 38–9
democracy of money, 47–8
democratic capitalism, 48
democratic centralism, 52
'depression cartels', 144
Descartes, René, 26

INDEX

Deuteronomy, 95, 97, 98–9, 103, 122
Dickinson, Emily, 30, 46
difference engine, 153
Diocletian, Emperor, 37
dispersed culture (Jews)
   business outsiders, 121–3
   usury, persecution and competition, 123–6
Disraeli, Benjamin, 32, 57
Doria, Lazaro, 100
Drucker, Peter, 7
dry exchange, 108–9
du Pont, Pierre, 31
Durant, Will, 31
Dutch merchant-adventurers, 77–9
duty, 1, 69, 72–3

East India Company, 78
ecclesiastical power, 64–5
economic debate, 20
economic man, 1
efficiency, 173
Einhard, 97
Einstein, Albert, 14, 115
Elias, Norbert, 87
Eliot, T. S., 14
elites, 134, 135, 141, 187–8
Elizabeth I, 109, 112
embourgeoisement, 124
Emerson, R. W., 186
employment (computer industry), 169–70
enabling information, 160
Enaudi, Luigi, 98
engineer-entrepreneurs, 95
Enlightenment, 105, 176
enterprise
   wisdom and, 15–16
   see also capitalism and enterprise;
     Christianity and enterprise
entrepreunership, autonomy and, 9–12
epilogue, 191–2
equality, 179–80
Erasmus, Desiderius, 15, 104, 115
eternity, computers and, 155–7
exchange, natural instinct and, 186–9
exchange economy, 76
exchange rate, 109
expert systems, 162

Factory Act (Japan, 1911), 138–9
fame, 9
fellowship, 176
feudalism, 72, 73, 75
   Japan, 127–9
flexible manufacturing, 171
Ford, Henry, 15, 31
Frankenstein's computer (story), 163–4
free enterprise, 112–16

freedom, 42, 43
freedom and accountability
   freedom as trust, 69–71
   honour above honesty, 71–4
French Revolution, 177, 178
Freud, Sigmund, 14
Friedman, Milton, 57
Fugger family, 109, 110, 159

Galileo Galilei, 14, 180
General Motors, 31, 172
generosity, politics and, 55–6
gentilhomme, 187
German Contract, 107
Goethe, J. W. von, 85
gold (and privileges of kings), 81–3
good faith, 63
Gorbachev, M., 50, 51, 52–3, 60, 179
government
   culture and, 183–6
   see also politics and business
Grand, Sarah, 24
Gregory, Pope, 59, 60
Gresham, Sir Thomas, 109
Gutenberg, Johann, 104

Hammarskjöld, Dag, 13
Hanseatic League, 158
Hearn, Lafcadio, 129, 130, 138
Heian empire, 128, 134, 176
Heinemann (publisher), 23–4
Henry IV, 82
historical debate, 20
Hitler, Adolf, 6, 179
Hollerith, Hermann, 168
Holmes, Oliver Wendell, 153, 154, 187
Homer, Sidney, 79, 103
honesty, 5–6, 15, 180–1
   honour above, 71–4
   Japanese, 131–2
honnête homme, 187
honour above honesty, 71–4
hopefulness, 11–12
Huguenots, 82, 111, 114
humanities, 85
humanity, 177–9

Iacocca, Lee, 29
ideas (that shaped business)
   capitalism and enterprise, 107–16
   Christianity and enterprise, 91–106
   preamble, 89–90
ideology, 47, 87–8
importance and urgency, 12
individualism, 42, 135, 186
industrial capitalism, 94–5

INDEX

Industrial Revolution, 67, 87
   Japan, 129–30
industrialization, 171, 172
industry and society
   gold (and privileges of kings), 81–3
   man and machines, 85–8
   steam age, 83–5
inflation, 97–8
information, computers and, 157–9
information age
   business computers and society, 167–74
   people, computers and business, 153–4
   preamble, 149–51
   symbol of, 167–8
information society, 137, 161
Innocent IV, Pope, 99
instinct, exchange and, 186–9
intellectual leaders, 13
interest, nature of, 97–8
interest rate
   Japan, 141, 142, 144
   nature of, 97–8
   overhead costs, 102–3
   universalism, 98–101
   usury, 43, 89, 95–7, 101–2, 123–6
   usury redefined, 101–2
Internal Revenue Service (USA), 38–9
International Business Machines Corporation, 168
international division of labour, 149
international division of management, 149–51
international division of trade, 149
international trade, 25
internationalism, 75, 115
intuitive leaders, 13
investment, 141–2, 143–4
irrationality, 29
Ishimoto, Shidzue, 129–30, 146
iugum, 37
Ivan the Terrible, 179

Japan, 119–20
   civility in business, 137–46
   clustered culture, 127–36
   negotiation art, 29–30
   Westering of, 142–6
Jefferson, Thomas, 39
Jerome, St, 73
Jews, 112, 115
   dispersed culture, 119, 121–6
John of Salisbury, 33
Johnson, Paul, 112,122
Johnson, Samuel, 47, 57
Jonson, Ben, 77
judgement, decision-making and, 16–18

jus mercatorum, 180
justice, 20–1, 179

Kakuzo, 131
kalos kagathos, 178, 186–7
Kant, Immanuel, 42
Keene, Donald, 119
keiretsu, 141, 145
Keynes, J. M., 42, 58, 142, 183
kings, privileges of, 81–3
kingship, 75, 76
Kissinger, Henry, 32
Klausner, Joseph, 121
knightly discipline, 134–6
knowledge
   -based society, 157
   computers and, 159–62
   judgement and, 16–17
Kohl, Helmut, 58
Kreuger, Ivar, 5

leadership, 5, 187–8
   management and, 13–15
Lee Kwan Yew, 58
legal tender, 64
Lenin, V. I., 19, 51, 65
Leninism, 49
Leonardo da Vinci, 92, 95
Levi, Peter, 183
liberty, 42, 43
   privacy and property, 58–60
Lincoln, Abraham, 181
Lloyd George, David, 57
Locke, John, 26, 92, 178
Lombards, 125–6
Louis XI, 82
Lovelace, Ada, 163
Luther, Martin, 92, 104, 109–10, 115
luxury goods, 66–7

machinery, 85–8
Maine, Sir Henry, 136
maintenance economy, 76
Malthus, Thomas Robert, 83
man
   computers as extension, 169–70
   machine and, 85–8
management, 31, 140–1
   international division of, 149–51
   leadership and, 13–15
manners, 137–9
manufacturing sector, 170–4
marketing (attributes of)
   negotiation, 28–32
   salesmanship (legends), 23–5
   salesmanship (styles/character), 26–8
Marshall Plan, 50

INDEX

Marx, Karl, 19, 93, 115, 131, 141–2, 191
Marxism, 46, 53
Mary I, 112
mass production, 66, 67, 82, 84, 143, 171
materialism, 185, 188–9
Matthew, St, 91, 92
Maximilian I, 65
Means, Gardiner, 60
mediaevalism, 101
Medici, 158, 159
Meiji Restoration, 119, 128, 136
mercantilism, 20, 52, 66, 67
 rise of, 75–7
mercantilists and adventurers
 Dutch merchant-adventurers, 77–9
 rise of mercantilism, 75–7
merchant-adventurers (Dutch), 77–9
merchant-salesman, 178
merchants (emergence as class), 104–6
Metternich, K. F. von, 32
military–industrial complex (Soviet), 49
minds (of man and machine), 164
Ministry of International Trade and Industry, 140, 144
money, 89–90
 democracy of, 47–8
 transnationalism of, 107–9
monopoly, 82
Montaigne, Michel de, 178
More, Thomas, 114
Morris, Ivan, 128
motives, taxation and, 35–40
movements (that shaped business)
 freedom and accountability, 69–74
 mercantilists and adventurers, 75–9
 preamble, 63–7
Mun, Thomas, 98

Nabokov, Vladimir, 115
Napier, John, 105
nationalism, 75, 86
nationhood, 73, 75
natural instinct, exchange and, 186–9
negotiation (art of), 28–32
Neumann, John von, 168
Newton, Isaac, 14
Nobility of Breeding, 177
Nobility of the Robe, 177
Nobility of the Sword, 176–7
nomocracy, 122–3
non-retail services, 172
Nonconformists, 77, 89, 114

oligopoly, 6
Oppenheimer, Sir E., 24
opportunity cost, 102
otherhood, 98, 101, 102

overhead costs, 97, 102–3
oyakata, 138

Pacioli, Fra Luca, 72
paper currency, 64
party apparatus, 49
Pascal, Blaise, 13, 180
patronage (of the arts), 177
Paul, St, 91–2
Penn, William, 178
people and computers *see* computers and business
perestroika, 60
perfection and perfectibility, 42–3
persecution, 123–6
personal attributes (in business)
 enterprise and wisdom, 15–16
 entrepreneurship and autonomy, 9–12
 judgement and decision-making, 16–18
 leadership and management, 13–15
Peter the Great, 179
Philip IV, 65
philosophical debate, 20
piepowders, 178
piracy, 178–9
Pirenne, Henry, 100, 125
Pliny the Younger, 41
political debate, 19
political power, 64–5
political and business
 politics around business, 45–54
 politics in business, 55–60
 preamble, 41–4
politics around business
 capitalism, 48–9
 communism, 49–51
 democracy of money, 47–8
 politics and business, 45–7
 Soviet Union (future), 51–3
politics in business
 conservation, 56–7
 generosity, 55–6
 liberty, privacy and property, 58–60
 reform, 57–8
politiques, 178
population, 83
 overpopulation, 87
'portfolio insurance', 161
power, 9, 64–5, 159–60
preux chevalier, 187
price
 architecture of, 21
 congruence, 6–7
 value and, 19–21, 188
prisoners' dilemma, 6–7
privacy, 176
 liberty and property, 58–60

production
  computers in, 170–4
  mass, 66, 67, 82, 84, 143, 171
productive information, 160
productivity, 173
property, 86, 92–3
  liberty and privacy, 58–60
Proposition Thirteen (California), 36
protectionism, 20
Protestant ethic, 109–12, 132
Protestants, 111, 112, 113–14, 115
Puritanism, 82, 111, 112, 113, 114, 185
'putting-out' system, 84

qualities, 188
quality circles, 142

rank, 179–80
Raskob, John, 31
rational speculation, 105
  idea of, 94–5
rationality, 29, 97–103
  missing links, 97–103
raw materials, 173
Reagan, Ronald, 58
reasoning, computers and, 162–5
reciprocity, 63, 64, 135
refinement, 176–7
reform, politics and, 57–8
Reformation, 77, 105–6, 109–12, 113–14
Rem, Lucas, 71
Renaissance, 105, 115
Rhodes, Cecil, 23
Ricardo, David, 83
rights, 69, 72–3, 92–3
ringi system, 140–1
risk, 10, 11, 17, 102
  rational speculation, 94–5, 105
Roman Empire, 37
Rothschild, Lionel, 158
Rothschilds, 23, 158–9
royalism, patriotic, 76
Ruskin, John, 74, 156

Sakharov, A., 53
'salami tactics', 101
salesmanship, 7
  legends, 23–5
  styles and character, 26–8
samurai, 135
Savary, Jacques, 72
Schama, Simon, 79
security, 10
services sector, 170–4
Shaw, G. B., 14
slavery, 81, 111, 178, 179
Smith, Adam, 19, 92, 93, 183–4

social change, 169
social equality, 179
social justice, 179
social security, 57
socialism, Soviet, 51–3
society, business in
  civilization, 183–9
  preamble, 175–81
  see also computers (and society); industry and society
Socrates, 161
Sogoro, Sakura, 128–9
Solzhenitzin, Alexander, 53
Sombart, 112, 119, 123, 176
Soviet Union, 51–3
Spindle of Necessity, 167
sprezzatura, 187
Stalin, Joseph, 49, 51, 179
standards, 1
status (in Japan), 134–6
steam age, 83–5
Stevin, Simon, 72
surplus value, 48, 93–4, 142

Tawney, R. H., 74, 88, 96, 109, 112
taxation, 73
  motives and, 35–40
  systems, 33–5
tea ceremony (Japan), 131
technical debate, 20
technology
  man and machine, 85–8
  see also computers (and business); computers (and society)
textile industry (Florence), 84
Thatcher, Margaret, 58
theocracy, 45–6, 52
theological debate, 20
Thomas, St, 41
thrift, 66, 83
Thurow, Lester, 170
Tocqueville, Alexis de, 136, 150
Tokugawa era, 135–6, 139
tolerance, 177–9
Tovey, Dr, 124–5
transnationalism (of money), 107–9
Trevor-Roper, Hugh, 105, 115
'trigger points', 160–1
triple contract, 107
trust, 63, 64
  freedom as, 69–71
truth, 131, 132
Turgenev, Ivan, 11
Turing, Alan, 168

Ulysses, 177–8
Underhill, Evelyn, 113

unemployment, 66, 93, 170, 173
United East India Company, 78
United States, 184–5, 187–8
unity (of business), 1–2
universalism, 75, 90, 98–101, 102, 115
urgency, 12
usury, 43, 89, 109, 110, 122
  idea of, 95–7
  nature of interest, 97–8
  persecution and competition, 123–6
  redefinition, 101–2
  universalism, 98–101
utilities, 66, 67

value attributes (in enterprise)
  price (architecture of), 21
  price and value, 19–21, 188
vertical integration, 94
Voltaire, 134

wages, 83
Weber, Max, 86, 113, 114, 119
welfare, 55, 57–8
Wesley, John, 116
West India Company, 78
westering of Japan, 142–6
Wiener, Norbert, 168
Will, George F., 57, 141
Wilson, Thomas, 43, 96
Winston, Richard, 73
wisdom, enterprise and, 15–16
Wolf, Heinrich, 65
work, idea of, 91–4
world trade, 173

zaibatsu, 139

Index compiled by Jackie McDermott